# CRITICAL THINKING

# AND MENTAL MODELS:

## THE GREAT COURSE TO EMULATE EFFECTIVE THINKING SYSTEMS OF THE MOST SUCCESSFUL LEADERS. THINK FAST, SET GOALS AND SOLVE PROBLEMS BY ADOPTING BRILLIANT STRATEGIES.

By reading this document, the reader agrees that under no circumstances is the author responsible for any losses, direct or indirect, which are incurred as a result of the use of information contained within this document, including, but not limited to, — errors, omissions, or inaccuracies.

Table of Contents

# Introduction

There are a lot of definitions of what critical thinking is. And that's what you should expect about it. Critical thinking includes much of what we are doing every time we use our brains.

The common words that describe critical thinking are: interpreting, observation, reasoning, cognitive process, reflective thought, rational thinking, focused thinking, analyzing, well-versed opinions, and evaluating information.

The aspects of critical thinking are evaluation, observation, judgment, problem solving to making conclusions and decisions. Critical thinking can also mean the ability to think conceptually while making conclusions.

The philosophy of critical thinking has started back thousands of years to the Greek Socratic and Buddhism tradition that include asking analytical questions to know if the claims to knowledge can be sensibly correct with logical reliability. When a person thinks critically, it is clarified as goals, evaluate evidence, examine assumptions, and evaluate conclusions.

In making hard decisions or choices, people that are engaged in critical thinking pay attention to the relevance of arguments and focus more on careful observation. They might not recognize the particular details in a new situation, but since they can consider details and explore it efficiently, they can deal with things that may frustrate others. These people can also normally solve problems and make decisions that require skillset.

Those who are able to maintain this type of perspective can undertake long-range tactical planning, instantaneously process details from different sources, and multitask. Along with outshining at troubleshooting themselves, they are able to serve as good listeners to those who are struggling with complicated or difficult problems. Furthermore, they can easily make an expectation of possible results of certain situations and have plans on what they are going to do next.

Some people notice the outcomes of progressive critical thinking without comprehending that it's what they are actually doing. Critical thinkers are usually the most creative people as they arrange and prioritize important matters before spending their time on useless activities. They usually work less long than most people. Quite the reverse, though they work less, but are likely to work smarter. They dig the deepest part of the most complicated issues and use calm scrutiny to make the right decision or solve a complex problem.

*Admit that your life isn't perfect and you are a very flawed person*

Just kidding, kind of. Actually, you have already done this part. This is the first step that life improvement requires. It is the very same reason why you have sought and obtained this book. This part serves as a congratulatory section for accomplishing the biggest step of all. Now, you should proceed with the small things you should do to enhance your life further.

*Don't take life so seriously!*

Yes, it is inevitable that people tend to look at life more seriously if they are having problems. But take note that nobody is forcing you to forget relaxing or laughing at your problems from time to time. Also, being serious does not ensure you that you will solve your life-related dilemmas faster. Therefore, do not use your hardships as an excuse to prevent yourself from having a good time.

*Do not live in the past – live in the present*

Dwelling on the past forever will prevent you from moving on and looking forward. You might never progress from your issue if you spend most of your time thinking about what you should have done in the past to prevent certain events from happening in the present. Yes, you might learn invaluable lessons from the past. However, you can learn those lessons quickly once you thought about it for two to three times. If you learned your lesson, immediately tell yourself to move forward and disregard the past. Then, it is time to think about the things that you should do to prevent new problems and fix your current situation.

*Do not procrastinate when it comes to problems*

Procrastination is not always a bad thing. However, when it comes to solving problems, nobody should procrastinate about it. Remember that if you leave problems on their own, they tend to multiply and become worse. As much as possible, immediately fix your problems whenever the opportunity shows itself.

However, it does not mean that you should just go ahead and apply any solution you come up with just to fix your problems quickly. Of course, you will also need to take your time when formulating the fixes you will use to eliminate your problems.

*Do not punish yourself because of the small mistakes you have committed*

Small mistakes are small mistakes. People tend to ignore them since they have no time to remember all those things in their lives. Do not punish yourself too much every time you create one; you will not get anything done if you do that. You have much more important things to do than to castigate yourself on every occasion.

*Do not expect too much from life*

Life is unfair, and it is true. Not all the things you hope for in this world will happen. Even though some are just within your grasp, there will be times that you will not get those things. It is typical that things go wrong unexpectedly. So, in case you experience some frustration just because you did not achieve something, let it go. You can just try again, or try something else.

*Step out of your comfort zone*

From time to time, you will need to explore beyond the boundaries of your comfort zone. Holing up in the same situation and place will only limit you in a small isolated place. Going out of that comfort zone will let you expand your horizons. Simply put, doing something you find uncomfortable will become comfortable if you do it at least once or more.

Avoid thinking that you are perfect, you can be perfect, or you aim to be perfect

Everybody is unique and special, but many people are not that special to become perfect beings. Even if you ask optimistic people, being perfect resides in the realm of impossibilities. Also, letting others know about what you think about perfection may make them push you away from them.

*Identify the things you should improve upon*

Of course, it does not mean that you should perform a total overhaul in your life. Imperfection does not mean that everything in your life is bad or every aspect of yourself is a failure. Find your weaknesses and imperfections and then come up with plans on how to eliminate them.

# Chapter 1
# An Overview of Mental Models

One fact of life that we just can't deny is that our brains will be responsible for everything that the body does. This means that anything that affects our brain will then affect all of the other facets of our lives. Yes, the brainpower is going to rely a lot on its software or the mindset that you have, and the hardware, which is going to be the nerves.

We know it is really hard to work with a system that is sophisticated, with lots of good hardware, and then have some bad software on it. This just ends up being a bit energy-wasting blend of silicon and metal in the computer. In order to help put these mental models into the proper perspective, it is important for us to take a look at some of the different elements that are at the core of this idea, and how we are able to use them to our advantage.

First, we need to take a look at what the model means for our "mental model". A model is simply going to be a microcosmic representation of the real object. This object can be either non-physical or physical, it really doesn't matter. It is going to be like a blueprint, a diagram, a mould, or a map and it is going to depict some of the key features of the real object, without having to bear all of the costs that come with this model being around.

Modelling is something that we are going to see in a lot of technological and scientific endeavours. However, this doesn't mean that we have to leave the models confined to only those two fields.

There may be a ton of different options out there that promise to work on getting things done more effectively, and a lot of promises that are going to try and help you to manage your time and more, but some of the best options out there for you to use are going to be these mental models.

You get to choose which one you use, and the more of them that you learn about, the easier it is to grab one out of your toolbox and put it to good work. This opens up a whole new world of what you are able to do, how easy it is to get tasks done, and how you will be able to succeed in any endeavour that you attempt to do. How many of the other options out there are going to be able to provide what these mental models will provide to you as well?

This does not mean that you can't use some of the tools that are out there and available to those who want to enhance the mental models. And if you are working on things like time management and want to use charts or diagrams or the Pomodoro timer to help you, then this is perfectly acceptable as well. But you will find that working with these mental models can be effective, even without all of the other equipment along for the ride.

There are a lot of core reasons why you may want to take a look at modelling and see how it can work for a lot of different technological and scientific adventures. Some of the most common reasons for this include:

- A model is going to help you to depict a mental concept, and this makes the model concept a lot easier to understand overall compared to the main concept.

- A model is going to make it easier and cheaper to present the real object to others.

- A model is going to be a lot cheaper to make and use than the real object. This means that the cost of creatively destroying the model if needed will be low.

- A model is easier to adapt to the changes in the main concept than the real object.

- These models are going to be cost-effective methods to avoid some bigger mistakes. Mistakes, faults, and even misconceptions can be easily detected when we look at the model and appropriate corrections done to it prior to launching the real object.

While it is true that there are some models that we are able to look at in physical form, there are others that do better when we look at them in virtual form. Physical models are going to be for objects that contain some form such as planes, cars, ships, buildings, territories and the like. Virtual models, on the other hand, are going to be for things that are not physical, such as the thoughts, imagination, senses, and interpretations.

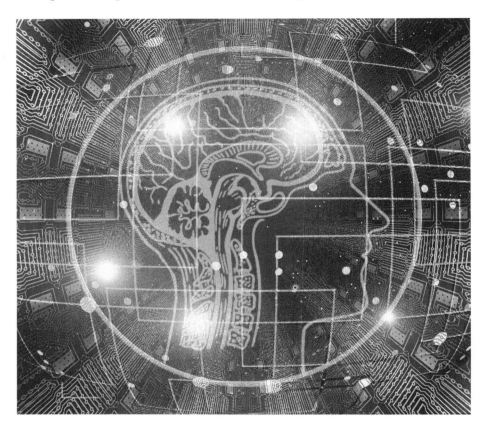

Mental models are going to fall within the virtual nature above because the mind is not really a physical object. Some of the virtual models that you may see that relate to this could be things like strategic military models, culture models, organization models, and more.

## What is a Mental Model?

With this understanding with us, it is time to take this a bit further and look closer at what a mental model is all about. A mental model is going to be a blueprint of how you can boost up the cognitive engine's capacity to make decisions that are more strategic and intelligent. A mental model is going to be just a one-dimensional view of reality. This means that if we want to make sure that we have a better view of multi-dimensional reality, you would need to work with more than one of these mental models at a time. When we are working on a real-life situation, we are going to not rely on a single model but will rely on a mental multi-model instead.

This brings up the question of why these mental models are so important. Just like software is able to help direct some of the functional behaviour that we see with a computer, a mental model is going to help to direct some of the functional behaviour of your brain, and because of that, it directs the rest of your body as well.

Using the analogy of the computer a bit more, you will be able to more easily see and deduce some of the core reasons that make it imperative to start using these mental models in your own life. Some of the biggest reasons why these mental models are so prevalent and such a great option for you to use in your life includes:

- They are efficient: A mental model is going to help the brain learn how to run more efficiently, especially when it comes to dealing with some tasks that may be repetitive and routine. This is going to allow the brain to be more creative and to focus on novel inputs instead.

- Effectiveness: These mental models are going to help limit the errors that we see, and will make sure there is less wasted effort. This is going to make the brain power more effective in delivering the outcome that you are looking for.

- Economy: This is a term that is all about the efficient and effective utilization of the resources that we have. the brain is going to need a ton of different resources to help it operate. In fact, you will find that the brain is the most resource-intensive organ in the whole body. Because of this, any increment to the effectiveness and efficiency of the brain means that you are going to use your resources more wisely.

- Certainty: The mental model is going to help you bring about some level of certainty when it comes to common challenges in your life. Because of this, a mental model is able to coordinate the brain function of several people inside the same team or group. This means that the model is going to bring in a bit of predictability that you need when it is time to handle challenges and more.

- Productivity: With certainty and economy added to the mix, the productivity that you will see with the brain is going to go higher. In the end, the productivity of not just the individual person, but also the whole team, is going to go up.

The neat thing is that these mental models are going to be able to do a lot of different things for you. They can first step in and enable you to see the world in a more accurate manner, and then you can use this new form of accuracy to predict the future in a much better way than it would have been without them. This model can also help you to form a new mastermind kind of alliance because you will then be able to find some people who can suit your model and then the connections that are built up from this are going to be mutually beneficial. These connections are important because they will sharpen up the mental model that you have, making them more precise. And finally, the mental model is going to help you to generate some breakthrough ideas because they will have a unique angle view of the situation that is at hand.

Another thing that we need to take a look at before we move on with these mental models is the origins of them, or how they got started. we are not able to tell with a great deal of certainty where these models begin with because it is believed they started at the beginning of time. while we are going to be able to create some mental models deliberately from our knowledge, it is possible to have some mental models that are created in a more instinctive manner.

For example, it is possible to have one of these models etched into the genes. It is going to be these that will help an infant learn how to respond to some of the external stimuli in a certain way that we can predict from the moment they are born. For example, all infants know how to respond to heat and light, how to identify their mother, how to suck, and how to cry, even though they had no chance to learn how to do these things. Over time though, the infant is going to develop some of their own mental models so they learn the best way to communicate and interact with their mother.

Because of this, it is believed that these mental models are going to be as old as humankind. We can call some of them primal mental models. But then there are the mental models that we can create for our own needs, the higher or the secondary mental models. These are the ones that we are going to consciously and deliberately generate out of our learning and some of the practice experiences that we have.

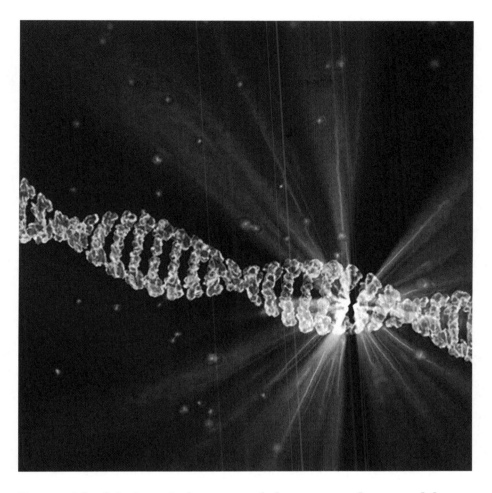

Even with this in mind, some of these secondary models are going to be etched into our genes after some time if we use them in the proper manner. This is done to help future generations learn how to cope and adapt with some of the changing environment that is out there. For example, epigenetics is going to be an interesting field of study that can help us to look this over a bit more as well. In this guidebook, while we recognize that all of the mental models can be important we are going to spend our time focusing mostly on the higher or the secondary models, the ones that adults are going to purposely create to help them make things easier.

## How Our Minds Work and Why the Models Help

To help us learn a bit more about these mental models, we first need to take a look at how the mind works and then how the models can come in and make a difference. The best first step that we can take to help understand how the mind works is to look at a computer model. A human-like robotic computer is going to be the closest that we can get to see how the mind works for now, so let's focus on that.

Using a computer model, there is going to be a part for the hardware, and a part for the software. The robotic computer is going to have what is known as the main body, which will include the torso and the head, as well as some limbs that are a part of the peripheral limbs. The thinking part of this kind of model is going to rest in the head, just like with us. Inside the head, we are going to see that there is a CPU, which is going to act as the brain of the computer. The visible part of this CPU is going to be the hardware and the parts that we are not able to see will be the software.

In the same way, the brain is going to have parts that are the software and then parts that are the hardware. The part that is the software is going to be the mind. We are able to see the mind as a type of container where our mindset will be able to reside. And the mindset is simply going to be a set of a lot of different software programs we use. Just like the software on a computer has several sets of programs that are meant to play their own role, this helps to make sure that everything functions the way that it does.

To clarify, the mind is going to be like the software. And the mindset is going to be the collection of a unique set of instructions or programs that will each tell the brain how to execute the specific functions that it should. When it comes to working with computer software, we do have the system software as well as the application software.

To start with the system software, this is going to be the part of the brain that will manage all of the internal functions of our mind, with regards to how it is going to properly manage any resources that it has. The application software is going to comprise different sets of programs, and each one is going to be designed to execute specific functions when it is triggered by some kind of stimuli that is external, such as the environment. Because of this, the Application software is going to be based on the environment that is around it. This could be more specific by talking about how to interact productively with the external environment.

The software itself, which is going to be our mindsets here, is going to be crafted more like an interface that works between the external environment and the internal environment. This software is going to be crafted based on a lot of different models. First off, the "System software" in the mind is going to be based on some of the internal things that we hold inside the body. Then the "Application software" is going to be crafted based on how the external model outside of the body is behaving.

However, we will see that the actual interface that happens between the two of these needs to be both external and internal features. They have to be able to work well together in order to get the mind to work the way that we want. The external model is going to be more dynamic compared to the internal one. The reason for this is because the external environment is going to be more dynamic and fluid, and this results in us needing more dynamism, adaptability, and flexibility in our application model.

This means that we need to make sure that the Application model is going to turn out multidimensional as if in a way to obey Adam Smith's concept of the many-sided man. This is the reason why we are going to have hundreds, if not more of these Application models, which are going to come about naturally because humans have a big desire to cope with the external environment that is always changing around them.

It is going to be on the basis of this multidimensional and many-sided perspective that this book is able to establish some of the foundations that we are going to work on. Our goal is to explore, dissect, and then synthesize some of the best mental models that are established, ones that have been put together to make it easier for humans to cope with the ever-changing environment that is all around them.

It is common for a lot of us to feel lost in the modern world, trying to adapt to things that are always changing and we may not always know how to deal with these kinds of situations. But with the help of these mental models, we can better understand the world around us, become more adaptable, make better decisions, and so much more.

## The Benefits of These Mental Models

There are a number of benefits that come with using mental models. This is why so many people enjoy using them to help make decisions easier, to help them with time management, and to make things easier overall. If you are someone who struggles to manage their time or to make some of the important decisions you need and even end up making the wrong decision in a lost of situations, then it is time to use these mental models.

The first benefit that comes with these mental models is that there are so many of them to learn about. There are believed to be hundreds of these mental models that you are able to choose from. While most of these are going to be variations on some of the most common mental models, you will find that you still get a lot of different choices when it comes to the kind of mental model that you need to use in different situations. You are not stuck with one or two models that you have to work with, and if you don't want to use one, and you don't like it, you don't get any options. Mental models come in a variety of types and choices, so you can find the one that works the best for you.

You will like that they can be customizable for your needs. You can take any of the mental models that we have in this guidebook, and customize them for your needs. We will take a look at a few examples of how you are able to change this around a bit, and use the same mental model in different manners along the way. This helps you to find the right mental model,

These mental models can work for almost any kind of situation that you need in life. We are going to take some time to look at many of the situations where you are able to use these mental models and the different types of mental models that you are able to use in the process. This will help us to see that no matter what kind of situation we encounter in our lives, we can rely on these mental models to help us out.

These mental models can make decision making easier. There are a lot of different types of mental models that you can choose from, and many of them can help you to really take control of the decisions you make. indecision is going to really cause us to fall behind and miss out on some of the best opportunities out there. We also worry that we are going to make the wrong decisions along the way, which can make it harder for us to know when we should slow down and when we can speed up when it comes to making decisions for every aspect of life.

Mental models are able to come into the scene and solve this kind of problem. They are set up so that you can eliminate the bad choices right away, or even learn how to go with one of the first options that you think about because these are often the best, and then just jump right in. We waste too much time with indecision and we make the wrong decisions because we just have too many options to choose from. With these mental models, we learn the right steps to take to get things done, and often this helps us to make better decisions than we did before.

Time management can become a breeze when you start to use these mental models for your needs. Do you struggle with being able to manage the time that you have in a day? Do you feel like you are working hard to do all of your work, but you get to the end of the day, and you are so far behind that you have no idea how you will get it all done?

Many people are going to struggle when it comes to time management. They feel like they are doing a lot of work, but then they are always behind and won't be able to get it done on time. Often it is more about taking care of the right tasks at the right time, minimizing the things that distract you, and getting your mind to stay on track.

The right mental model is going to make this happen. We will talk about a lot of different types of mental models that can work to make you more efficient, to help you get more of your work done quickly and to keep you on track. Utilizing these don't only make your work easier, you may find that you can get the work done, with a little extra time, helping you to leave work with nothing left undone, and less stress overall.

Mental models can be a great addition to your life because they can really change up your view of the world. And often this is in a positive manner. Too many times we spend our efforts concentrating on things that take too much time, debating against too many decisions, and even dealing with procrastination. These mental models are going to come into play because they help us to take control over these problem areas, and focus our attention on how to get things done, and get them done in a quick and efficient manner.

And with all of the different options that you are able to work with when it comes to these mental models, you are sure to find the one that works the best for you, no matter what kind of situation you are dealing with. Think about how much easier your life can be, and how much more you can get done on a regular basis when you are able to implement these mental models in an effective manner.

## Mental Models Affect the Way that You Are Going to View the World Around You

It is important to remember that these mental models are going to be a unique way to look at the world. They are going to be a set of tools that you are able to use to help you think in a more effective manner. Each mental model is set up in a manner that is different, with a framework that helps you to look at life, or even at an individual problem that is coming your way.

While there are a lot of ways that you are able to work with mental models, you will find that they really shine when you use them to develop more than one manner to look at the same problem. For example, let's say that you would like to make sure that you avoid procrastination and make sure that your day is more productive.

If you understand some of the different mental models that we will talk about in this guidebook, then you are going to have a range of options that you can use to determine your priorities, and actually get things done.

Remember here that one mental model is not necessarily any better than one of the others. It just depends on which one you like the most, and which one seems to be the best for you. These mental models are going to work to give you a large range of options that will help you determine your priorities while getting important things done in the process. When you have a lot of different mental models available to use, it is easier to pick out the one that is going to work the best for your current situation, rather than only using the one that you have learned how to use.

## Law of the Instrument

According to Abraham Kaplan, the Law of Instrument is going to be important. This one is going to be based on the idea that if you give a hammer to a young boy, then the boy will establish that everything coming on the way will require pounding. We can look at this in a similar manner as if you only have one framework for thinking about the world, then you are going to try to take each problem that comes to you into that framework, and that doesn't always work. But if you have a set of mental models to work with, your potential for finding a solution is going to increase.

One thing that is also interesting with this one is that the problem you are facing is going to be vividly evident as you increase your expertise in a specific area. It is dangerous to specialize in one mental model since you will over-rely on it and such will be leading to your downfall.

This is why we need to work to have a larger set of mental models, you are going to better your capacity to solve a lot of problems. This is because you provide yourself with a variety of collections for obtaining the answer that is right. When your toolbox is full of lots of different mental models, you will be better set up to choose the best tool for the given situation. The more mental models you have to work with, the greater your range and variety of thought and as a result the more the opportunities you are able to identify.

# Chapter 2

# The Detailed Overview about Critical Thinking

Unfortunately, there is no distinct definition of critical thinking. This is fitting because the very nature of critical thinking frowns upon monopolization. That said, critical thinking is the process of independently gathering information, analyzing, synthesizing, and evaluating the information in a bid to form decisions, decide what to believe, and how to act upon that information.

Critical thinking is a character trait, i.e. it is easy to discern a critical thinker from a non-critical thinker by analyzing a few key traits present in how one behaves, acts, and carries him or herself. While each critical thinker is different and exhibits different character traits, below are the most significant character traits present in most critical thinkers.

## Understanding Critical Thinkers: Innate Character Traits

Critical thinkers use the critical thinking skills to analyze information, determine which aspects of information to believe and which to disbelieve, as well as how to act upon that information. As such, all critical thinkers must:

## Be Open-Minded

As a critical thinker, you must not stick to what you know; instead, you must allow yourself a chance to learn new things, and new ways of doing things: You must be and remain open-minded at all instances. This trait will allow you to give proper attention to other ideas without showing bias, which often prevents you from seeing other options and possibilities.

## Be Well-Informed

Critical thinking revolves around making informed decisions. You cannot make informed decisions based on scanty information or knowledge. As a critical thinker, you must prioritize information gathering. If your knowledge on a specific subject is lacking, desist from making a decision, and proceed to gather relevant information (become well informed) on it before making a decision.

## Have Good Judgment

Critical thinking is more than listening to people's opinions; it is also about good judgment, i.e. the ability to sieve received information and determine if the said information is credible or not. Critical thinkers judge the credibility of information sources, the quality of arguments, and any evidence supporting an argument or information in question.

## Be Able to Develop a Position

Do not be tempted to confuse critical thinking with 'someone sitting on the fence'. As a critical thinker, you must develop a position. You should be able to think (critically of course) about issues, come to your own conclusions, and be able to defend your position whenever the situation arises.

## Clarify Issues, or Ask for Clarification

As a critical thinker (or a practicing critical thinker), you must be able to clarify your position or your points. You can do this by explaining your points in a systematic manner, and answer any questions that may come up when you voice your position on an issue.

As such, you must develop the ability to ask questions that implore others to clarify what they are saying. When you cannot understand what someone is saying, you cannot come to a reasonable conclusion in relation to the information that a person gives you.

At the end of the day, most situations will warrant that you come to a specific conclusion. It is important that as you draw conclusions, you exercise caution when drawing those conclusions. By exercising caution, when new information becomes known, you will be able to analyze it, synthesize the information, and do an evaluation.

Always remember that critical thinking is a nonstop process. If you discover new information that shows situations in a different light, examine this new information and decide whether it changes, or shapes your opinion on a subject.

Having looked at key character traits every critical thinker, you inclusive must develop, let us look at, and understand why critical thinking is such an important life skill.

## Why You Should Become A Critical Thinker: Importance of Critical Thinking

Critical thinking is not limited to a particular field or a particular group of people; it transcends domains and continents: everyone has the ability to engage in critical thinking. However, due to one reason or another, many of us often fail to utilize this ability. To give you the motivation to become a critical thinker, let us look at the importance of critical thinking.

## 1: Promotes Creativity

Creativity and critical thinking are two pieces in a pond. Here is how the two relate. To come up with something new, or to make something old better, you first need to study it, and form an opinion or idea on how to go about it.

You will need to research in a bid to understand which functions your creation will have, and how that creation will solve a problem or meet a certain need. Critical thinking helps you ask the difficult questions. It helps you come up with the best products and put forth your best efforts. Critical thinking allows you to 'think outside the box'.

## 2: Initiates Self-Reflection

To achieve growth, and live a meaningful life, you must shine light on what drives you, what is important to you as an individual, and how that relates to the world at large. Critical thinking enables you to reflect on your values and the values of your decisions. You will not 'hide from yourself'; instead, you will engage in self-evaluation, which will go a long way in helping you determine choices and decisions you make in your life.

## 3: Sets the Foundation for Science

Without critical thinking, it would be impossible to make advancements in science and technology. When it comes to questioning theories and searching for answers (thinking critically), scientists and researchers are at the forefront. Over the years, 'we' have discovered new methods of doing things, and improved upon old methods. Science relies on critical thinkers to come up with formulas and answers; it relies on data and proof of concept, concepts that call for critical thinking.

## 4: Allows Democracy to Flourish

True democracy flourishes when individuals can voice opinions, ask questions, and seek answers. Democracy provides governmental checks and balances; it allows citizens of a country to hold their leaders accountable.

Democracy cannot flourish in silence; after all, we have varied opinions. Critical thinking allows individuals to state their opinions and listen to the opinions of others, weigh these opinions, and arrive at a peaceful solution.

We often fight not because we disagree but because we feel as if our concerns are being neglected or trivialized. Critical thinking allows people from all occupations to look at issues from various angles, and arrive at the best possible solution.

## 5: Fits In With the Global Economy

Long gone are the days when batter trade of goods and services with neighbours was the 'it' thing. Today, the world has opened up to accommodate anyone with the means to communicate with buyers and sellers. Today, companies and organizations are constantly looking for new markets in a bid to stay in business.

However, due to cultural differences, political climate, geography, among other things, new markets present new challenges. Critical thinking enables companies and individuals to find ways to overcome such challenges, engage in global business, and make profit.

## 6: Enhances Presentation Skills

Life may call upon you to give a presentation at work, school, at a seminar, during a course, at a religious gathering, or even at a family meeting. To give a great presentation, you need to employ critical thinking. Critical thinking equips you with the skills to give clear and systematic presentations where you state your points, give the reasoning behind your points, and provide proof for your stand on specific subjects. By using critical thinking, when called to do so, you are also able to defend your position. When giving a presentation, you should use various resources such as graphs, charts and images to get your points across.

The importance of critical thinking cannot be overstated. As an individual, you must make enhancing your critical thinking skills a priority. To do this, you can use proven strategies to enhance your critical thinking skills.

## The Building Blocks of Critical Thinking

For decades, decision making has been bilateral in nature, in that it was either 'black' or 'white'. This means that decision makers would staunchly believe that something was right or wrong. Modern times have introduced a new angle to decision making, one that takes into consideration the fact that there could be several shades of grey. Arriving at these shades of grey is not simple, as a certain amount of logic, relevance and analysis is considered. At the core of the process is critical thinking.

There are many ways one can define critical thinking. Some say that it is the process that begins with the conceptualization and application of information. This goes on to analysis and evaluation of said information, and from this, a belief is formed or an action taken. To get the information, one needs to observe what is happening around them, relate this to a specific experience, reflect on the outcome and communicate their final decision. Critical thinking can be applied to a host of the subject matter.

Another definition states that critical thinking requires certain skills including honesty, rationality, open-mindedness, discipline, self-awareness and judgement. With all these in mind, it becomes possible to analyze data in order to arrive at a conclusion.

One more definition refers to critical thinking as a way of expanding the way one thinks, in a bid to improve the quality of their thoughts. This calls for considering a subject or an issue and then analyzing and assessing it, using self-motivation and self-discipline. The result of critical thinking is the ability to see things from various points of view and have a clear and precise solution to problems, as well as being able to communicate these solutions effectively to other people.

These are just some of the definitions that exist for critical thinking, though they do have some things in common. To begin with, one must see things differently, looking at them in more detail before making a decision. This requires the information that is available to be deeply analyzed and researched, and once all the information has been considered, it becomes possible to take action. Critical thinking thus is the best way that one can arrive at an informed decision.

## When Do You Use Critical Thinking?

These broad definitions may leave you wondering when you should actually use critical thinking. Would it be better when faced with complex decisions, or on a day to day basis? The truth is, you can use critical thinking at any time or situation, as it is so flexible in its applications. When making your decision, you will consider your critical thinking skills that will lead to certain responses.

## Critical Thinking Skills

Critical thinking does not occur automatically, as it needs motivation to move it forward. It also requires the culmination of special skills that together are able to bring about magnificent and well thought out results. The primary skill that you need is analytical. This skill enables you to look at a situation or scenario, and then break it into several parts, so that you can understand the nature of the situation, its function, and any relationships that it may affect.

Following analysis, you need the skill of applying standards. As you do so, you should be able to make judgments, based on certain criteria. These criteria could be personal, social or professional in nature. From the criteria that you select, you need to be able to discriminate, so that you can tell whether there are any similarities or differences in the situations that you are trying to understand.

The next skill that is needed deals with seeking information from a reliable source. This information should be holistic in nature, covering both historical and current data, as well as being both objective and subjective. The information will be scrutinized using logical reasoning, where an inference or conclusion can be appropriately supported.

These skills will bring you towards two final skills, which are predicting where you envision the plan that you are working towards and all the consequences that could result, and transforming knowledge, which change the form of your condition so that it can be relevant in a new scenario.

You can use these skills when you are creating a strategic plan, writing an article, brainstorming or using creative thinking for a task, making a scientific deduction, asking questions to arrive at a viable solution, or when making an argument on ethics. Critical thinking is the best way to ensure that your point of view is well received and backed up with the right information.

A look at these skills helps you understand the layers that are involved in making a decision or judgment based on critical thinking, and understand why it is necessary to develop these skills over time. A critical thinker needs to have the wish to go through information in detail and follow concrete evidence before arriving at any conclusion. These critical analysis skills should be mastered first, then, combined with the right attitude towards deep thought and inquisitiveness, critical thinking becomes possible.

## Why Do We Need Critical Thinking Skills?

If you have never thought about critical thinking in detail before, you may be asking yourself why you need to have any critical thinking skills in the first place. Well, when it comes to problem solving, using critical skills is the best way to arrive at a logical and supported conclusion.

When you do not use critical thinking skills for problem solving, then you will find that it is easier to fail from making terrible decisions. Problem solving calls for making a decision while taking into consideration an element of risk. Through critical thinking, this risk can be analyzed so that all outcomes are thought of and anticipated, making it possible to deal with any consequence that results. It is like going into battle knowing that win or lose, you will have a way forward. Other benefits that come from critical thinking include:

## Effective Communication

Once an issue has been critically analyzed, it becomes possible to effectively communicate the right solution. This is especially relevant when the issue at hand is complex, requiring deep and intuitive thinking that is based on problem solving.

## Asking the Right Questions

To get the best solution to any situation, you need to be able to ask the right questions, in a way that the question is both clear and precise. With critical thinking skills, you are able to logically reason through all possible variables, so that the question asked is supported by viable information.

## Opens Up the Mind

Critical thinking makes it easier for you to be open-minded, as you learn to evaluate alternatives and understand the assumptions and implications of a situation. When you have an open mind, finding the solutions to problems that are complex in nature becomes considerably easier.

Critical thinking helps you to reason in a logical way, as well as to make wise decisions and solve problems.

# Chapter 3
# Why Bother with Critical Thinking?

Why learn to think critically? Because the world is a much more complex place than it was even ten or twenty years ago. The rise of technology has given rise to the need for individuals to work harder to search for the truth. This is because we are bombarded with a wide diversity of opinion on most every issue we face as humans and as citizens. Let's examine a few of these controversial issues so that we can get a sense of the value of being able to think critically about them:

## Our Global Environment

Does human-generated activity influence the climate on our planet? Does the pollution put out by our factories and automobiles here on Earth damage our atmosphere to the degree that this damage will eventually cause mass flooding and devastating weather incidents?

Many scientists believe that the human race will eventually destroy itself if we continue to use carbon-based fuels such as oil and coal, and yet many others are of the belief that the earth's atmosphere is so complex and influenced by so many variables that there is nothing man can do to damage it. Both sides have examined climactic and atmospheric data over the course of the years. The controversy exists because both sides interpret the data differently. In other words, even though they are viewing essentially the same information, both sides are making assumptions about that data, and drawing conclusions and formulating implications based upon that data, that are very different.

Consequently, we as consumers of mass media and news are presented both sides of the argument and are then expected to make important decisions about what, if anything, should be done about this concept of global warming. Generally speaking, liberal politicians in the United States support the belief that global warming is something that should be addressed now, as opposed to later. In fact, in 2006, former presidential candidate Al Gore produced and narrated a movie called "An Inconvenient Truth," in which he purported the effects of global warming and advocated for immediate plans and action in order to reduce the threat. On the other side of the argument, represented by mostly conservatives in the U.S. and elsewhere, there is a strong belief that while climate may be in a state of change during the last ten or twenty years, it is a natural change, one of many that have occurred since the beginning of time. Adherents of this argument are of the belief that man has no control over climactic changes and money spent on the effort to reduce greenhouse gases is money wasted.

To most people, this argument may not seem important, but decisions regarding the concept of global warming have the potential to affect all of us. People who have worked in coal mines and in oil refineries are affected because if efforts to seek alternative energy sources are ramped up, their jobs could be affected. Already, many coal miners have been put out of work in the U.S. as the popularity of cleaner energy sources, such as natural gas, solar power, and wind power, have been developed and put into operation. As coal mines have closed in parts of the United States, people move away from those areas, and those trends mean that other industries that support that area will suffer as well.

As a critical thinker, your mission is to examine the information available to you regarding global warming, if in fact you view this as a potentially critical issue. There are essentially two ways to do this: one is to get the data from those who have studied it and interpreted it, and the other is to find the raw data and interpret it for yourself. Which of these methods do you think would be easier? Which method do you think would allow you to develop a more accurate picture of the problem, or lack thereof?

## Government

As I write this in the fall of 2016, the United States is in the midst of a critical presidential election. Although mass media spends the majority of its time and energy focusing on the candidacies put forth by the Republican Party and the Democrat Party, there are many other parties represented by candidates that are vying for recognition in the presidential election as well. The Republicans and the Democrats get most of the attention because they have been around for a long time and they are supported by millions of people and millions of dollars in the United States. Does that make them any more likely to be more effective to hold leadership positions in the United States government? This is but one of the questions for critical thinkers to consider as they work to decide who to support in the November election.

Many voters in elections tend to focus on the individual candidate, which is not always the best strategy for choosing an elective office-holder. Candidates not only represent themselves; rather, they represent the parties that support them as candidates, and those parties more often than not have very different ideas about how government should work and what its priorities should be. Although it is certainly important to get a sense of what candidate appears to be a stronger leader or has better ideas, keep in mind that they do not work by themselves to get the country's business done. Critical thinkers do their research on what the candidate's party represents and what policies they do and do not support.

Critical thinkers are sceptical about all the information that is presented to them by virtually any source. This is not to be taken in a negative sense; it just means that practicing critical thinkers do not take information, particularly information put out by governmental agencies, at face value.

Although government is based upon the premise that it is in existence to protect citizens from hostile forces and to serve by offering a wide variety of services, critical thinkers are well aware that people that make up government often have their own agendas that directly contradict the mission of protecting and serving the populace. Politicians usually desire to remain in office, and for that reason, often they may say or do things not because they are true, but because it is what they think the public wants to hear.

## Mass Media

Mass media can be defined as any means of communication that is intended for vast numbers of people, including television, cable, radio, newspapers, magazines, podcasts, and the Internet. We have seen shifts in the level of influence these components of mass media have enjoyed over the past several years, most notably the rise of the influence of electronic media and the decline of the power of newspapers and magazines. In addition, with the onset of multi-channel media such as the Internet and cable television, we have the opportunity to be exposed to a much greater variety of opinion regarding topics than we ever had prior to the development of these media.

Is all of this information a good thing? This question is relevant because such a wide array of data requires consumers of the information to work harder to get to the truth. We must remember that people who put forth opinions on issues are usually doing it because they are attempting to persuade their audiences, and truth-seeking consumers need to be aware of the mechanics of argumentation so that they are able to assess and evaluate the arguments being put forth.

The problem with all of the information available is that most people have no idea how to evaluate arguments, and purveyors count on the ignorance of their audience members. Critical thinkers pay attention to the context in which mass media reports their news stories, as well as the arguments they use in order to get their points across.

## The First Step as a Critical Thinker is to Reflect Upon the Way You Think

Have you ever taken the time to think about the way that you think? It's an interesting concept, isn't it? We are involved in conscious thought pretty much all of the time, and yet most of us spend very little time actually reflecting on how we evaluate information or how we decide what we are going to say or what we are going to do.

## Reflective Thinking

Critical thinkers understand the value of reflective thinking and utilize the practice regularly. One cannot be a practicing critical thinker until he commits to practicing introspection, which is defined as the examination of one's own mental processes. Introspection allows one to indulge in an exploration of one's own mind. Here's an exercise that you can use to get started in reflective thinking:

Before you go to bed, set aside five minutes to ponder the following questions:

- What was the best part of my day today and what made it so good?

- What was the least enjoyable part of my day today and what could I have done in order to make it not feel so negative?

- What did I do today that pushed me toward accomplishing my goals?

- What was the best thing that happened to me today?

- What did I learn today?

- What made me anxious or stressed today? Why?

- What should I have accomplished today that I failed to accomplish?

- Did my activities today reflect my core values and my goals?

- Did I invest in my relationships with others today?

- By doing what I did today, what did I choose not to do?

# Chapter 4
# Changing Mental Models for Instructors

What is the mental model? While you can discover a few depictions in an Internet look, a standout amongst the best meanings of a mental model is the accompanying:

A unique set of convictions and strategies to translate a given setting; more often than not supported by a less-cognizant worldview or perspective.

The setting is somewhat of a bad word, however, for our motivations consider setting all things encompassing your educating condition. Today the customary mental model of how teachers approach the learning circumstance is under increasing scrutiny.

This is the same old thing as there have dependably been incredible discussions over instructive strategies. We presently have something new to consider - contemporary scientific research on how the mind learns. While not convincing, this research underpins the test of the customary "instructor tell" approach.

As a consequence, teachers and educators in every single instructive setting are exploring different avenues regarding various techniques for instructing students. Teachers are receiving new technologies without additionally looking at their very own conviction frameworks about what comprises successful educating specifically and how the world all in all functions.

If you trust a world without structure and request prompts tumult, how dedicated would you say you are probably going to be to surrendering a whole class to assemble talk strategies, pretends, and re-enactments?

You may trust students ought to have something to do with what it is they realize, yet feel caught by the pioneer's guide you should pursue when leading a workshop. Your perspective does exclude adaptability in managing request and structure every once in a while, how likely would you say you are to search for approaches to join understudy association in the current structure?

It is conceivable to change one's mental model, yet when you initially comprehend what it is. When you are in a domain where an accentuation on understudy focused learning has made you feel like an outside onlooker to the procedure, you should need to consider changing your mental model about compelling education and the instructor's job.

For a specific something, if you think teachers need to give structure and request to a learning domain, check the works of the dad of effective instruction, John Dewey, and you will discover did as well he.

In this day and age, shouldn't something be said about embracing a half and half model - one that fuses the best of the requirement for structure and request with the best of dynamic investment from the students.

If your pioneer's guide contains different pretend and reproductions, let the members select the ones they feel suit them best. If time licenses, break members into dialog gatherings and let them build up their very own pretend and recreations.

Audit whatever address notes you have with an eye toward active understudy cooperation. Time is dependably a down to earth adversary in an imaginative homeroom, however, search for opportunities to pepper your addresses with accounts and work precedents drawn from the encounters of the understudies. Search for appropriate opportunities to interfere with the address with open-ended, intriguing inquiries.

- Mental Models: The Box Everyone Is Trying to Think Outside of

How frequently week after week completes a businessman hear, "It's a great opportunity to do some outside box thinking?" Mental models are the case everybody is attempting to get away. Mental models forestall thinking forward occasions. Individual points of view are built through discernment, creative energy, and understanding of the world. An individual sees a sweet treat and is sure it is a piece of candy or is it a mobile phone with a

64

confection case? The original mobile phone case was a lucky reasoning forward occasion since it deconstructed a psychological model. The undeniable utilization of mental models is to an individual's perspective on her or himself in connection to the environment. Self-idea is built through apparent abilities, social undertakings, and instruction. Quite a bit of this self-idea prompts intuitive assumptions.

Human assumptions overflow into a business. Most organizations flourish with remaining in front of the challenge and comprehend that when lack of concern sets in, the upper hand will be lost. Business pioneer assumptions lead to comfort, which makes rearrangements of the real world. Frequently these assumptions render companies stuck in a similar spot as advancement cruises them by. Great multi-channel companies are mainly influenced by this marvel as representatives and the executives become increasingly more disconnected from the more prominent corporate mission. Cross-lattice worldwide companies, specifically have notoriety for having turned out to be agreeable. "This is how it's dependably been done," is expressed again and again as companies lose a piece of the pie to concealed challenge and development.

The tale of the large organization that disregards ground-breaking occasions and is in this manner undermined by the minor, yet deft, the contender is told again and again in business schools. The solution for foolish assumptions is a portion of the outside box thinking. Outside box thinking can make the most prominent companies deft in their essential leadership. People are inalienably defective and need support foreseeing future business slants because of assumptive mental models. The picture of rivalry around an organization, which workers build, is a model. A reasonable decision for any organization is the option of picking outside box thinking as insurance against lack of concern, brand value misfortune, and client whittling down.

## Try not to Wait Until You Need Corporate Emergency Triage.

Sometimes the most out-of-the-crate thing an organization can do is search outside for assistance to develop a superior sort of various. Outside the organization, however, outside the business. As much as your organization or association needs a development expert, you likewise need one that comprehends importance as the establishment and venturing stone, not an idea in retrospect.

Each industry and friends has its very own way of life, and that culture frequently delivers a sort of "conventional target visual impairment." Similar thoughts keep coming up because the same individuals are entrusted with thinking of new answers for old issues.

## Mental Modelling - Things You Should Know About Thought Chains

Contemplation is the way toward understanding one's claims mind, intending to follow your Thought Chains to make a usable Mental Model.

Our psyches are dynamic always. As we associate with our condition, our minds are continually making mental idea chains. This prompts a ceaseless blast of commotion. It resembles having a radio station, set to a similar channel, playing in your mind for time everlasting. Without the advantage of volume control or an on-off switch, you are lost. Yoga and Meditation give you volume control and an on-off change to utilize at whatever point you have to.

The majority of our thoughts and activities are made from these psychological idea chains. We are indeed what we think. So then it pursues that we ought to consider seeing how the mind functions, seeing how our very own personalities work, as something critical and to is paid attention to very.

It bears rehashing; this is the thing that reflection does. It is a procedure that depends on a working model of how our psyches work. Contemplation is a procedure that enables us to get ourselves. Through reflection you can:

- Look at your musings,

- Look at your reflections from the eyewitness and the watched,

- Learn how to change how you think, to be increasingly beneficial,

- Realize that the style in which you believe and interface with the world, decides how glad or tragic you are, lastly,

- Realize the many physical and mental advantages that yoga and reflection gives.

Mental action makes musings that are connected with different considerations. So, for instance:

- You see somebody that helps you to remember an old companion named Bob,

- You think," I genuinely like Bob,"

- You wonder what Bob is doing,

- You wonder how the old pack is getting along,

- You wonder if Bob is on Facebook,

- You continue to look at Facebook, to locate your old companion Bob and the majority of your other old companions from the group.

So the underlying collaboration with the earth triggers a particular activity. This is usually the situation. First, you respond to the individual that helps you to remember Bob. You react to the outside natural improvement. You, the onlooker, at that point, continue to watch the boost and respond. This activity triggers one more idea and perception and response, and one more and again.

You may even make thought chains that will, in the long run, lead to a shocking idea example or topic. For instance:

- You begin seeing the individual that helps you to remember Bob,

- You know that you "like" Bob,

- Bob makes you feel better,

- You think, "Sway was dependably fit as a fiddle, he generally practiced a great deal,"

- You consider you claim physical moulding,

- You see that you aren't exceptionally cheerful about the shape that you are in,

- This makes you feel severe,

- You think, "I need to get to the rec center and exercise harder."

- You at that point watch, this makes you feel better. However, you genuinely don't have sufficient energy to get to the exercise center today around evening time, since you need to work late,

- You at that point see that you feel ineffective that you won't most likely work out today around evening time.

In the above idea chain, you went off point, and you may have seen, that you went from feeling better to feeling terrible to feeling better, to feeling awful once more, all inside a couple of minutes. Wow! Insane right.

However, this is actually what we do regularly. We always subject ourselves to this unproductive mental move. Moving to start with one chain of musings then onto the next, frequently without monitoring the result for us.

You have no clue how to stop it, change it, or possibly not to have it negatively influence you. Sometimes you'll even carry on without acknowledging what you're doing.

Through Yoga and Meditation, you will figure out how to screen your psychological idea chains and perceive ineffective mechanical examples in your reasoning. You will frame a working model of how your mind capacities, with the goal that you can without much of a stretch, see negative idea ties and start to make new, positive considerations to supplant them. You will push ahead with your life and show a fulfilling and lively reality.

- For Great Ventures - The New Mental Model For Post-Recession Success

The world has significantly changed since the Great Recession that started in 2008. We never again live in a universe of saw dependability and sureness. We live in a universe of saw shakiness and uncertainty, and many have anticipated that it will remain that path for quite a while. We are exceptionally all alone ventures, whether we remember it or not.

The two definitions I like best characterize an endeavour as

1.) an undertaking involving uncertainty with regards to the result, particularly a hazardous or dangerous one and

2.) a business venture hypothesis in which something is gambled in the expectation of benefit.

Amid this Great Recession, most all that we did livelihood or side interest moved into the domain of being an endeavour by these definitions. There was considerably less conviction, more hazard or peril, and we needed to continue forward with more trust in progress than the likelihood of accomplishment.

We presently live in an endeavour based world. Grasping that worldview or viewpoint puts you in a space that builds your chances for progress. Then again, when you obstruction this new reality, you increment your danger of disappointment as we discover our way to recuperation!

In any case, it isn't just your prosperity that depends on this new mental model, yet your bliss too. Tony Hsieh constructed his most recent organization on the reason of "conveying bliss." In request to convey satisfaction through his organization, Tony invested a lot of energy at work and home exploring joy. In this manner, he chose to compose a book and make development on "conveying satisfaction."

What indeed strikes me about his point of view and the use of his viewpoints on joy is that he takes a gander at it from the endeavour-based outlook. He is a serial entrepreneur who has expertly fabricated various incredible ventures. The exercise he gained from his first endeavour (that he sold for $265 in 1998) was that achievement was not so sweet as it could be without joy. He was hopeless in the later phases of his first endeavour and along these lines resolved to make satisfaction a piece of his next ventures.

Seeking after Great Ventures is tied in with seeking after both inexhaustible achievement and extraordinary joy! Given Tony Hsieh's examination and application, satisfaction includes:

- Seen Control

- Seen Progress

- Connectedness

- Vision/Meaning (being a piece of an option that is greater than yourself)

- A portion of these is similar segments required for inexhaustible achievement.

Grasp incredible endeavour based reasoning, and you will end up being the administrator and controller of your predetermination in the post-subsidence economy. You will likewise encounter a lot more noteworthy achievement and bliss on your journey!

- Sales Leadership - Building a Shared Mental Model

The job of a Sales Leader is to interpret the association's vision, mission, and qualities into a significant setting that sales groups can identify with and feel energized by. If this is accomplished, at that point, the Sales Leader will have made a sales group with a mutual mental model. This changes a collective sales group into a high performing one.

**For clarity, here is a concise depiction of the accompanying terms:**

- An association's vision is a managing picture of accomplishment shaped regarding a gigantic objective. It is a portrayal in words that invokes an image of the association's goal. A convincing vision will extend desires, yearnings, and execution. Without that incredible, appealing, significant vision, why trouble?

- A mission statement conveys the substance of an association to its partners and clients, and the inability to state and impart an association's mission can have hurtful results around its motivation.

- As Lewis Carroll, through the expressions of the Cheshire Cat in Alice in Wonderland says, "if you don't have a clue where you're going, it doesn't make a difference which way you go."

- Core values are the result of a mission statement that is proposed to educate or shape all consequent essential leadership, which additionally gives regulating criteria permitting approach creators to acknowledge, dismiss or alter arrangement intercessions and exercises. They are a directing arrangement of thoughts that are verbalized, comprehended, and bolstered by the association's workforce.

- Qualities are convictions that the association's workforce hold in like manner and try to try. The classes manage their presentation and the choices that are taken. In a perfect world, a person's close to home estimations will line up with the spoken and implicit estimates of the association. By building up a composed statement of the opinions of the association, people get an opportunity to add to the pronunciation of these qualities, just as to assess how well their attributes and inspiration coordinate those of the association.

- The Human Capital Development Model, made by Krauthammer International, is a quick procedure that can take top administration ideas, and interpret them into a setting that has real significance for staff at all dimensions.

**The way to breathing life into this model is to respond to the accompanying inquiries:**

- Does my group comprehend the association's vision and how their job draws the association nearer to accomplishing it?

- How can my sales group interpret the association's mission into one that applies to them?

- How do the association's core values sway on the everyday obligations of sales individuals?

- Which of the association's qualities does my sales group identify with?

- How would we be able to translate these qualities, so they turned out to be convincing for every deal individual?

# Chapter 5
# Major Mental Models

Mental models don't just affect our thoughts, they also influence our actions. We use mental models every day even when we are not consciously aware of it. With just a few mental models at our disposal, we are bound to develop familiar patterns of behaviour because our thoughts and decisions will be limited to the range of mental models we have. In this case, when challenges arise, we will inevitably fall back on old patterns to try and solve them or resign ourselves to coping with them.

If you cannot think in new ways or change your belief system, it becomes difficult to see new opportunities or overcome existing challenges. We are surrounded by aspects of biology, physics, psychology, and many other disciplines. We exist in a multi-disciplinary world where different elements coexist to form a functional ecosystem. It is therefore important to have knowledge of the big ideas or major models in the different disciplines.

For instance, if we look at the law of reciprocity in physics which stipulates that for every action there is an equal and opposite reaction; it may have its basis in physics but it cuts across all aspects of life. Knowing that for every choice you make there will be a consequence that makes you consider the outcome of your decisions with the outcome in mind in effect making your decisions better thought out.

Models such as reciprocity indicate that from reach body of knowledge there are key ideas and mental models that we should have in our repertoire if we are to have a truly comprehensive understanding of the world and how it works. Restricting yourself to an area of specialization limits your options, opportunities, and ability to adapt to an ever-changing world.

When you develop a broad range of mental models, each model builds upon the other and interlink based on related concepts. These linkages create a latticework of mental models making a more effective system of thought and filtering information. The development of mental models involves the integration of acquired knowledge and experience. This integration enables inferences to be drawn from past experience.

Experience forms an important component in the structure of mental models. Mental models are necessary for the comprehension of situations and systems. By creating simplified internal representations of complex external systems and occurrences, mental models enhance our understanding of different phenomena and how they work.

Mental models influence how we think by;

- Organizing knowledge and information in a way we can understand it.

- Creating reference points from past experiences.

- Linking related concepts to create procedural knowledge.

- Mental models enable us to predict possible outcomes of different scenarios through mental simulations.

## Mental Models in Psychology

Mental models influence our thought and decision-making processes. We tend to draw conclusions based on our beliefs, prejudices, emotions, and experiences. This means that our perceptions are biased dependent on individual our beliefs. These beliefs influence our perception by predisposing us to see things in a way that confirms the beliefs we already have. In this case, it becomes difficult to change our thought and behaviour patterns because we adopt rigid or set beliefs that we use to judge and assess situations, people and systems.

## The Ladder of Inference

The human thought process takes place in less than a second so it is difficult to realize our default reactions because they occur instinctively. We each give meaning to our observations and then base our actions on the meanings we have derived. The ladder of inference as developed by Senge illustrates a seven-step process of thinking and reasoning.

We select facts from our experiences and different events. These facts and observations based on the meaning we assign to them, form the basis of the assumptions we make regarding the event. From these assumptions, we then make conclusions that ultimately form our beliefs and values system. We then proceed to act based on the beliefs we have created. This thought process from observation to action occurs at a subconscious level. It occurs repeatedly every time we are exposed to stimuli.

*The Peter Senge ladder of inference is illustrated below;*

| | | |
|---|---|---|
| Step 7 | | Actions |
| Step 6 | | Beliefs |
| Step 5 | ⬆ | Conclusions |
| Step 4 | | Assumptions |
| Step 3 | | Meanings |
| Step 2 | | Selecting facts |
| Step 1 | | Observation |

The conclusions we make typically reinforce our beliefs, which will in turn influence the facts we choose to select from our observations. This means that we will ignore certain facts and focus on bathe facts that are in alignment with our beliefs. This means that the conclusions that we will draw and resultant actions will not be objective but rather biased because we let our beliefs influence what we see. This is why perception is subjective and two people looking at the same situation can draw two totally different conclusions of it.

To avoid making biased decisions we can use the ladder of inference to track back to our beliefs and evaluate how they influence our observations and conclusions. By going back to the previous step and questioning your conclusions, you can identify loopholes in your reasoning and thoughts and in effect evaluate your conclusions and assumptions. We will often jump to conclusions quickly in the process missing important facts and ultimately making bad decisions.

Applying the ladder of inference can help you follow a logical reasoning process that will enhance the effectiveness of your reasoning and lead to better decisions.

To limit the influence of our personal beliefs on the assumptions and conclusions we make, we can make a conscious effort to challenge our instinctive reactions by;

- Increasing our level of self-awareness which can be achieved by taking the time to analyze our emotions and thoughts and what triggers them.

- Increasing our level of social awareness by; this taking time to recognize and understand the views, emotions, and attitudes of others

Changing our belief systems and developing new thought patterns by developing our set of mental models is the most effective method to shape our realities through our actions and behaviour. Mental models in psychology are ideas and thinking concepts that we can apply to increase our aptitude for solving problems and generating ideas. These include:

## Understanding Your Circle of Competence

Each of us through education, experience or natural aptitude has useful skills and knowledge in certain areas. Some of us are gifted in arts such as music while others are great in chemistry.

Our circle of competence is comprised of the areas in which we are good at both at a personal and social level. Knowing whether your abilities are in a particular field and how you can fully exploit these abilities is a key factor in achieving personal development and success.

Spending time and energy pursuing things that you are not good at can cause frustration, poor self-confidence and lack of motivation. In the same way that success breeds success, constant failure can lead to a lack of motivation and drive leading to more failure. When you find that your pursuits are consistently ending up in failure it might be time to evaluate your circle of competence in relation to your pursuits.

**Self-awareness** is the crucial key in identifying your strengths and weaknesses. Being aware of what you are good at, where you need to improve and what motivates you are the key ingredients required for personal development. Developing goals and objectives that play to your strengths gives you the opportunity to make the most use of your skills and natural abilities. Identifying your circle of competence will enhance your sense of purpose and give you a clear direction on what to focus on and pursue.

## First-principles of Thought

Using a first-principles approach to think basically refers to breaking down a process to its basic components and concepts. A first principle is a basic assumption that cannot be broken down any further. It involves looking at a situation at its foundation and starting from the known facts then building from these basics.

When we understand the first principles of a system, we can deconstruct it and then construct it again more effectively. These principles allow us to avoid imitations by not following what has already been created by others but allowing us to build our own systems and conclusion by deconstructing existing concepts then using the core elements to create something new.

## Inversion

Naturally, we are inclined to plan for what we want to happen. If you want to be a doctor you go to medical school, when you want to win a marathon you train your body for the event and so on. The principle of inversion is thinking about what you want to achieve in reverse by considering what you don't want to happen.

For instance, if you have to speak in public you can focus on the mistakes to avoid rather than focusing on how to give a good speech. Using this approach, you can easily identify the obstacles that would prevent you from giving a good speech. In this case, if you avoid using jargon, being repetitive or not having a clear message you will inadvertently give a good speech by simply focusing on what not to do.

Using this method when making decisions and solving problems, you can effectively avoid procrastination or unlock solutions that may have seemed out of reach. By eliminating obstacles, we clear the path to achieving the goal intended.

## Second-order Thinking

Second-order thinking requires us to consider our actions, the immediate consequences of those actions as well as the long-term effects that are bound to arise as a result of the choices you make. The question, "and then what?" directs second-order thinking.

In a hypothetical situation where you are torn between finishing your assignment and going out with friends. When you weigh the options of staying in and finishing your paper or going out with your friends for a drink, going out would seem more gratifying. However, if you ask yourself "and then what" you would be likely to realize which of the two options might have negative consequences.

Thinking beyond the immediate outcome of a decision to the consequences is crucial in making decisions that have lasting positive effects and in ensuring that we are not destructed from our long-term objectives.

## Bayesian Method

The Bayesian method is a theory-based on statistics where probabilities express the level of belief in the occurrence of an event. When this principle is applied to thoughts, it involves is a thought considering all probable outcomes and scenarios. When we add new data onto the pre-existing probabilities and update them, we create a more realistic expectation and can thus make decisions based on the expected outcomes. Constantly updating our field of probabilities means that we can create more realistic simulations of scenarios and possible outcomes. We can then use this insight to make decisions that are in alignment with the desired outcome.

## Mental Simulations

We can use hypothetical scenarios to anticipate what will happen. Mental simulations aid us in predicting the probable results of our actions. By running these simulations, we can use the predictions arrived at to determine the best course of action in any given situation. We can effectively use mental simulations to not only anticipate future events but also to prepare for what will come in the future.

## Occam's Razor

The Occam's razor principle is a problem-solving principle. It eliminates improbable option and asserts that usually, the simplest explanation is often the correct one. it encourages us to focus on what works and avoid getting bogged down by complex theories. Wasting time and energy contemplating complex scenarios may be counterproductive and frustrating. Basing decisions on simpler logic and proven fact scenarios limiting the margin of error. Occam's razor principle encourages us to trust our first instincts.

## Hanlon's Razor

The principle of Hanlon's razor is built around focusing thoughts on finding solutions to a problem rather than finding fault or someone to blame for the existence of the problem. When we apply this principle to our reasoning and thinking process, we do not attribute bad situations to malice but rather to a lack of knowledge. Devoting energy and time to the paranoid pursuit of people to blame for bad situations means that we do not focus on the solution.

## Major Mental Models in Key Disciplines

## Mental Models in Physics

There are many mental models in physics that have varied applications in various systems and are widely applied in other disciplines as well. These models include:

## The Law of Reciprocity

This law of physics stipulates that for every action there is bound to be an equal and opposite reaction. This is a multi-disciplinary law that applies not only in physics but also in biology, human behaviour, and many other fields. We can use this law to evaluate and make decisions with the consequences of these decisions in mind.

Life is a series of choices that we need to make on a daily basis. The sum total of these choices shapes our present behaviour and future outcomes. All the choices we make have consequences in both the short term and the long term. Using the law of reciprocity, we can make better choices by evaluating what the effects of our choices will be in the long run.

## Relativity

This theory has multiple applications in different contexts in physics. The most widely used concept from this law, however, is the fact that an individual is incapable of fully comprehending a system of which they are part.

A person in a plane may not physically feel the motion of the plane but an observer can observe the movement that is occurring.

Similarly, in personal situations when a person is in the middle of an event or situation, they cannot judge it from an objective perspective because they are immersed in it and can only see it from one perspective. To objectively judge a situation, we must first remove ourselves from it on a mental level and access it from an observer's point of view.

## Thermodynamics

The law of thermodynamics is also known as the law of conservation of energy and it describes energy transfer within a system. This law stipulates that energy cannot be created or destroyed in a system but that it is simply transferred from one form to another.

## Velocity

Velocity refers to the measurement of speed that occurs in a particular vector or direction. The addition of vector or direction. Using this principle in our lives can help us map out our progress in different spheres, by having a clearly defined starting point and destination in terms of objectives, we can assess our progress. Being able to determine if you are making progress or not can aid you in making changes to ensure that you are on the path to achieving your objectives.

## Catalysts

A catalyst is defined as a substance that speeds up a chemical reaction but remains separate from the reaction itself. Catalysts can be found in everyday life situations as well as in science. Identifying catalysts that we can use in daily life to accelerate our progress and advance our goals can help us in attaining our objectives and accelerate the rate at which we are able to achieve them.

## Leverage

Many innovations in engineering have been based on the principle of leverage. Leverage is a principle that is used to identify means by which heavy loads can be lightened and in effect make work easier.

## Inertia

The law of inertia states that a body with no net force acting on it will either remain at rest or continue to move with uniform speed in a straight line. Inertia is a basic physical principle of motion. Inertia minimizes energy use by limiting motion and action.

## Mental Models in Biology

The laws of biology apply to all living things, from single-celled living things such as yeast to multi-cellular organisms such as human beings. Some of the key models in biology include:

### Adaptation

To survive in their environments species of animals and plants must either adapt or die. Natural selection eliminates the weaker species in an ecosystem and allows the stronger ones to survive and breed. This natural process effectively ensures that future generations carry the best genes from the available gene pool.

The capacity to evolve and adapt to different circumstances and environments is an important element in human existence. Adaptability is a key element for success and growth since change is an inevitable part of life and our ability to cope with it will ultimately impact on personal development.

## Replication

Replication is the basic law of biology that ensures the continued existence of a species through multiplications. Replication is the natural process through which old generations create new generations and in effect ensure the continuity of life. Without replication or multiplication species would cease to exist.

## Self-preservation

The natural instinct to self-protect is present in all life forms. Animals develop defense mechanisms to help them survive adversity and protect themselves from predators. The self-preservation instinct is also present in humans. Our instinct for self-preservation affects our thoughts, behaviour, and relationships with others.

## Evolution

Evolution is one of the principal laws of biology. Mutations, gene selection, and natural selection ensure that species change over time to cope with their changing environments and habitats. Survival in nature typically favours those that are best equipped for the current circumstances in their ecosystem.

Evolution occurs through natural selection processes such as gene mutations.

## Hibernation

A wide variety of species have been observed to hibernate seasonally. When conditions are hard or unfavourable some species will go into a state of physical inactivity and resume activity when the season suits them. The main purpose of hibernation is to preserve mental and physical energy while avoiding unnecessary exposure to adverse conditions.

## Competition

Competition is a common phenomenon in all species. Natural resources are limited so there is an ever-present fight for the few available resources. Survival creates competition for food, water, and habitats. The strongest usually survive because they can get enough resources to sustain their existence. The human race is also subject to this law of biology. In a race of limited resources and opportunities, we exist in a constant state of competition amongst ourselves and also with the other living things that we share the planet with.

## Incentives

An incentive is the expected reward that comes after the completion of a particular task. All living beings including humans and animals are naturally incentive-driven. Predators hunt because they know they will get food at the end of the chase. Equally, we work hard to get rewards in terms of money, power or social status. Incentives work as a motivating force and as a justification for effort. Without incentives, it is hard to generate the necessary drive and motivation required to accomplish tasks.

## Cooperation

No one species in nature exists in isolation. Interdependencies and relationships are a natural element of an ecosystem. Cooperation is bred by the need to survive and exist in harmony with each other. The interdependence of species is crucial for harmonious existence. Humans also need each other to survive and make the best of their living situations. Cooperation and competition co-exist in nature and both are necessary for species to survive and thrive.

## Social organization

Social organization is a natural instinct evident in various animals across species. Groups of lions, elephants, apes and many other animals exist in structured societies that have leaders. This hierarchical organization of members within a group creates order in their societies and creates well-defined roles for each member of the group. Leaders of packs are expected to provide guidance, resolve conflict and provide protection for the other group members. Humans are not exempt from this law.

## Ecosystem

Ecosystems are comprised of groups of different life forms co-existing together in the same habitat. Habitats typically host different organisms that exist either in competition or cooperation with each other. Co-existing in these ecosystems are living organisms ranging from the top of the food chain to the bottom of the food chain. Without these ecosystems, a lion would not be able to find food because they would not have prey as part of their habitat.

## Models in Human Judgment and Behaviour

Mental models direct our thought processes and influence our actions by directing how we interact and relate to people, situations and systems. Some of the models that influence our behaviour include;

## Pavlovian Association

Pavlovian association refers to conditioning of the mind to associate an object with a pure conditioned response. Emotions are our knee jerk reactions to external stimuli. They are basic elements of human experiences. We have emotional reactions to both physical objects and the intangible associations of the objects that we create.

This principle has been employed with the creation of powerful brand identities where certain names inspire the confidence of the consumer. For instance, the brand name Apple is instantly associated with quality even before we use or test the product.

## Bias

Our belief systems and values mean that we often see things in a way that confirms our beliefs. We cherry-pick facts when observing a situation so that we highlight those that reinforce our beliefs and discount those that disprove our beliefs. Human perception is naturally biased because we tend to see our perspective as "right" and the other person's as wrong if it contradicts ours.

## Denial

Denial is the coping mechanism we employ when we are unable to process negative situations or emotions. The inability to acknowledge our failings, mistakes or bad decisions reduces our level of self-awareness. This in effect undermines our competencies on a personal level and when it comes to working and job performance.

## Safety in numbers

Nature has designed us as a social species. We coexist, interact, and form relationships with other people on a daily basis. This natural instinct to seek safety in numbers and communities drives us to cooperation and creating social structures that keep us in contact with others. Our desire to socialize and seek community is an inborn trait and is the basis for forming sound relationships and societies.

## Curiosity

Curiosity has been referred to as the mother of invention. This is because our desire to figure out the unknown drives us to consistently seek out new ways of doing things and new experiences. Without curiosity, we become content in the way things are. The universe is a large and dynamic system and we can only learn more and understand more when we actively seek out knowledge, opportunities, and ideas.

## Envy

Human beings are covetous in nature and are prone to desiring what belongs to someone else. We get jealous when we think someone has something that should be ours or that we think makes them have more than we do. Envy is a negative emotion because it focuses on what we do not have rather than what we do have.

## Availability bias

Out of sight out of mind is the basic principle that describes the availability heuristic. Our brain gives prevalence to the things we are in contact with frequently, what we deem important and the habits and actions we engage in repeatedly. These become easy to recall as they are always at the fore of our minds.

The availability bias is a natural brain mechanism to conserve energy by storing mostly information that is deemed as important. When we want to form good habits, we are encouraged to repeatedly carry out the desired action on a daily basis until it becomes instinctive. This method works because repeated actions are kept in the fore of our minds and with every repetition, they get easier and easier to do.

## Representative heuristic

We form opinions based on past experiences or generalizations of systems or people we deem similar. This results in stereotyping. Stereotyping means that we make sweeping assumptions about systems, people or experiences based on a single entity that we assume to be representative of the group.

Stereotyping impairs our objectivity in judgment by making broad assumptions and jumping to conclusions about a group that may actually have significant distinctions among its members. This is a common human weakness that leads to negative emotions and prejudices such as bigotry.

## Fairness

Our sensitivity to fairness has made the pursuit of justice a key part of the human social systems. We establish structures to ensure that things in social and workplace environments are done fairly. Our sense of justice changes with time and evolution of cultural norms. What was deemed fair and just yesterday may be regarded as unfair in the present.

Practices like slavery were at some point in history deemed perfectly legal yet are presently seen as an abuse of human rights. Time and exposure shape our values and beliefs and as such our concept of what is fair or justice constantly shifting.

## Survivorship bias

History more often than not favours winners and our interpretation of the past gives dominance to those we deem to have succeeded. We cherry-pick the stories that go down in history by exclusively focusing on the victorious and ignoring others who may have played equally important roles in history. This is why it is commonly said that no one remembers the person who came second.

## Confirmation bias

Pseudoscience exists because they cannot be proven to be either right or wrong. We tend to believe and see what reinforces and confirms our beliefs. Fields like astrology play on this tendency by offering insights into the future that can neither be proved nor disproved.

## Assumption bias

We tend to categorize people based on their behaviour without considering the circumstances that cause them to act in a certain way. An addict may seem like just a self-indulgent person with no self-control while in actual sense they may just be a normal person who went through a bad situation and is coping with it the only way they know-how.

Good people are sometimes driven to doing bad things by bad circumstances. Classifying people as either inherently good or bad based on isolated actions leads to the formation of judgment based on half-truths and opinions rather than facts.

## Relative satisfaction

Our levels of contentment are more often than not related to past experiences or the perceived contentment of our peers. We compare ourselves with the people around us and are more likely to feel content in our achievements if we feel we are doing better than our peers or at least on an equal footing with them. This is driven by our competitive nature which makes us feel the need to outdo each other.

## First impressions

We usually make up our minds about something or someone within a few minutes of coming into contact with them. Relying on first impressions too much can be misleading. Taking the time and effort to understand someone before drawing conclusions may save you a lot of misconceptions and false assumptions. Judgments that are based on surface characteristics are often flawed and inaccurate.

## Mental Models in Engineering and Mathematics

### The margin of safety

The margin of safety in engineering refers to the ability of a system to withstand loads greater than expected. The main idea in this principle is to protect yourself from unforeseen circumstances and challenges by building a buffer between your expectations and what could happen in reality.

### Normal distribution

The principle of a normal distribution is commonly used in statistics. This law is also used in social sciences to represent random variables whose distribution is not known. The central limit theorem states that averages of observed samples converge in distribution to the normal. Physical quantities that are expected to be the sum of many independent processes often have a normal distribution.

## Power laws

Stipulates that changes in one quantity triggers a proportional change in the next quantity regardless of the size of the quantities. One will always vary proportionately as the power of the second.

## Redundancy

In engineering, redundancy is the duplication of critical components of a system with the purpose of increasing the reliability of the system. This duplication is usually in the form of a backup that is geared towards improving the performance of the system.

Redundancy has two main forms. These are passive and active redundancy. Passive redundancy uses excess capacity to reduce the impact of failure on the components. On the other hand, active redundancy eliminates the decline in performance by monitoring the performance of individual devices.

## Regression to the mean

Long deviations from the average will tend to return to the average mean with the increase in the size of the sample under observation. Regression to the mean can deceive us into confusing statistical probabilities with causal probabilities.

## Algorithms

An algorithm is an automated set of rules defining a series of steps or procedures that result in the desired outcome. It is stated in the form of If- then statements. Algorithms are widely used in computing but are also evident in biological systems.

## Network effects

A network's value increases with the addition of nodes to the network. This principle is referred to as the network effect. It stipulates that some concepts are only as useful as their ability to connect with other concepts to increase functionality. This model also has very wide applications in various systems that require linkages for optimum performance.

# Chapter 6
# The Role of Mental Models

After looking into some of the best mental models you can find, it is imperative to delve into the role of these mental models. Certainly, this is something that might have crossed your mind as you wonder how the models will help you. So, why mental models? What makes these models relevant in your life? Of course, you now know that mental models allow you to understand how this world works. The varying models provide you with clear-cut information on comprehending how different thought processes can boost your thinking capacity.

However, it is still worthwhile to question yourself why and how these models can have a positive impact on how you think and perceive the world around you. Looking at the array of mental models, it can be argued that mental models can assist you to solve your problems faster. Challenges are part of our daily lives. This is what people have to go through to achieve their goals whether in the short or long run. To ensure that people achieve their goals, decisions have to be made. Accordingly, mental models come in handy to make the decision-making process easier.

In relation to what has been said, mental models, therefore, can act as guides toward the design of the approach you will be taking to handle a particular situation. In business, it will help you and your team to settle for an optimal strategy to solve a problem. The same can be said about your relationships. If there are problems you are facing, mental models can guide you on the best approach to take.

When Jeff Bezos was in a dilemma as to whether to start Amazon, he looked for a framework that would guide him to make the right decision. As such, he came up with the regret minimization framework. Using this framework, he pictured how he would feel in the future depending on the decision he made. In this case, he had a good feeling about starting Amazon and he was sure he would not regret the decision to quit his job and start the company. Therefore, his model provided him with the motivation he needed to easily and effectively make a sound decision.

From Bezos's example, there are three things that we can notice here. First, the regret minimization framework he used gave him confidence in the design he was using. He had the courage to make a big leap to start Amazon. You should bear in mind that he was a senior vice-president at the company that he left. So, he was not quitting because he was not earning well. For that reason, quitting his job was not easy. Without confidence, this is something that he would have just brushed off.

Secondly, the framework that Bezos used provided him with clarity. After coming up with his model, it was now clear that he would regret not implementing what he had in mind. The framework gave him a reason to understand that this was the right direction to take.

Third, Bezos's framework was rooted in the idea of focusing on the long-term consequences of a particular decision. He envisaged himself 80 years after starting Amazon, and he was sure that he would regret if he didn't work on his vision. Clearly, his mental model gave him a reason to believe in the continuity of his strategy.

Therefore, the advantages of using mental models in your life can be summed up as follows. It helps you gain:

- Confidence in your approach

- Clarity in direction

- Continuity of strategy


## Confidence in Your Approach

We live in a world full of uncertainty. You can never be sure about anything that you want to do. However, this doesn't mean that there is nothing that you can do to make your decision-making process simpler. Using mental models gives you confidence that the approach you are using has been proven and tested by other successful people in society. Once your mind acknowledges the fact that your framework is based on solid research, you will have the energy to pursue that which you have been thinking of. This is because you are more convinced that it will work. You have solid proof and nothing can stop you.

Besides, if you are working with a team, the mental models that you use allow them to believe the approach that you plan to use. In a way, when they comprehend how your approach works, they will grasp your understanding of the solution and embrace it.


## Leverage Luck and Intent

Since we agree that the world is full of uncertainties, it means that there is room for luck in what we do. Basing our argument on the probabilistic thinking mental model, numerous variables will contribute to succeeding in anything you do. Believe it or not, luck is one of them. The funny thing is that most individuals would want to attribute their success to certain facts. They will give plenty of excuses to justify that the decision they made was accurate. The reality of the matter is that luck influences how we succeed.

When using mental models as a way of improving your thinking abilities, you are more comfortable to open up to the world of possibilities. That's not all, you will also acknowledge the variables that contribute to your success. Simply put, you will embrace the uncertainty that this world puts you through.

Accordingly, mental models will be the right tools to steer you in the right direction.

Mental models provide you with the evidence you need to rely on your approach. They are a language that you can read and understand. Language helps you to communicate with other people. It gives you the ability to interact with others and to know what they feel. In the same manner, mental models are a language that you can master. The good news is that, you will not be the first person to use them. Thousands of people are using these models to solve their problems with ease.

## Differentiate Between Solutions

Undeniably, the more models you grasp, the more informed you will be. For you, it will be easy to distinguish between solutions that can be reached by using these models. At some point, you will realize that there are some models that provide similar solutions. The point here is that models give you the advantage of perceiving this world from different perspectives. Hence, you will not be limited to one solution. You can decide to utilize distinct frameworks to solve the diverse problems you might be facing.

## Accept that Ideas Match Needs

Another good thing about mental models is that it provides you with the right platform to confirm that your approach is ideal. In this case, when using any mental model, you will embrace the notion of a higher level of thinking. For instance, prior to making any decision, you will want to compare your decisions to what renowned scholars would do if they were in your situation. Eventually, this puts you in a situation where you make decisions based on what you have validated to be realistic.

## Avoid Politics

The confidence that you have in your approach will prevent you from second-guessing. You know what is right and what is wrong. Therefore, you will want to choose the best path with proven track record. Certainly, this is important, more so when working in groups. Some individuals might want to engage in trial and error to solve their problems. With your knowledge and expertise on mental models, this is what you will want to avoid. Making wild guesses on what you should do can easily bring any successful business to the ground. A mental model would save the day as it would provide the best form of interpretation to decide on what you ought to do.

## Clarity in Direction

In addition to giving you confidence in your approach, mental models will also provide you with a clear direction on how you should think and act. Throughout your decision making process, you will want to have a clear strategy on how you do things. The people around you should notice that you have a different approach to solving your problems.

## Engage in the Whole Experience

There are numerous situations that you will be faced with in regard to decision-making. The problem that you deal with today might not be the same problem that you handle tomorrow. Regardless, if you have mental models to turn to, you will always emerge victorious.

## Use Your Approach to Your Advantage

Looking at Maslow's hierarchy of needs model, there is no doubt that people love to feel good about their achievements. Meeting self-esteem and self-actualization needs will give you a reason to be happy about yourself. Mental models will steer you to make the right decisions that impact your life positively. The compounding effect that you will gain from your achievements will boost your self-esteem. Clearly, people will respect you. They will look up to you for assistance whenever they feel stuck.

Thus, your sense of direction in life will give you an added advantage as you will accomplish some of your personal needs as argued by Maslow's model.

## Transform Yourself

There is an overall transformation that will be taking place in your world. People around you will be the first to notice that you have changed. As you take your time to learn more about mental models, you will advance your knowledge. You will garner a deeper insight on how the world works. Accordingly, it will not be a daunting task for you to make sound decisions.

It is also worth noting that your metamorphosis will be evident through the life's goals that you will be achieving. Indeed, making the right decisions and succeeding in your ambitions go hand in hand. For that reason, you will be glad that things seem to work your way. This is the power of mental models. It delivers you results in remarkable ways.

## Continuity of Strategy

A continued use of mental models will provide you with a sense of advancement in how you do things. Besides finding it easy to make decisions and solve problems faster, your new way of thinking will help you gain better control of your life. Most of the decisions that you will be making require you to look into the future. Oftentimes, you will want to consider the long-term consequences of your actions instead of just paying attention to short-term gains.

## Mental Models Will Help You Change Gradually

At the beginning of this manual, we pointed out that transforming your decision-making process is a lifelong journey. It is not something that you can do overnight. There are numerous mental models that you need to comprehend to become a good decision-maker. The learning process will also not be complete if you fail to put into practice what you learn. Therefore, you must practice the new thinking frameworks that you will be learning from this manual.

Practice makes perfect. You don't have to be an expert in applying mental models to how you think and approach your problems. However, with constant practice, you can polish your critical thinking skills.

Simply put, mental models provide you with the frameworks that you need to make informed decisions in your life. Their role is to bestow you with confidence that your approach toward making certain decisions works. Oftentimes, we are skeptical not knowing the best moves that we should take. This is a common experience more so when faced with big life's decisions. However, with the help of these models, you can understand life from varying perspectives.

To gain the best from these models, you should equip yourself with knowledge by learning how to apply distinct models in the problems that you face. The more you know, the better. We live in a complex world and for you to grasp a solid understanding of how things work, it is vital that you have several mental models in your thinking toolbox.

# Chapter 7
# Cognitive Bias

When you are in the middle of a mental model, moving and shifting the vision of the completed project or outcome, you are causing all of the pieces to fit together perfectly. In the optimal situation, the only information flowing through your head would be the facts given and the processes necessary to come to a conclusion. However, we have human brains, and they don't just store facts and processes like a computer would; this is where cognitive bias plays an instrumental and often damaging role in our choices and the flow inside of our mental models.

A cognitive bias is essentially an error in the way that we think that affects our decision making skills as well as our judgment. One of the first ways that it is affected is through our own personal bias. Memories that are stored in our brain of a similar event that may have created a bias will lead to that altered bias thinking and decision making. These biases could throw an entire process off, leading to a choice that is not in the optimal range for the mental model.

Another cognitive bias that we struggle with is our attention span. In a world filled with distractions, technology, and a constantly evolving movement, it is easy to lose that attention when processing through your mental model. These distractions can also create biases that are subconscious. For example, if you are creating a grocery list, going through the financial steps, the listing, and the decision process, and you hear a commercial for a specific brand of cereal that may affect your choice. You may remember eating cereal as a child, the memory floating back through your head. That memory could invoke an emotion that will ultimately sway your decision making based on emotion rather than fact.

Think about how many different thoughts flow through your mind at any given moment. While just sitting around reading this book, your mind will pick up on cues from the words, spiralling outward. You may have just thought about your favourite cereal, having to do your grocery shopping, or even circumstances that you have related to your own life. All of these things come into your mind like noise, distracting you from the facts and the choices that you are presenting yourself within your mental models. Why is it that we do this? How exactly do we get so easily distracted?

## How Does Cognitive Bias Work?

We know that cognitive bias is an error in our thought processes while we are processing decisions, interpreting new information, and setting up the base of our mental model. The whole world can act as an error in our thinking. Our brains, regardless of their power and capabilities still have limitations to them. When you have a million things going on in your mind, your brain begins to shut down or block certain parts from your conscious thought. It is attempting to simplify the process of quantifying the information that you are trying to focus on. The problem is, your brain doesn't know which information is pertinent and which is not when you are thinking of a million different things.

That processing is supposed to help you make sense of your task, and of the world as it relates to it. Your brain also knows you are trying to make these decisions in a short amount of time. There are always deadlines in life, and we can't just sit here and let them glide away in our brains forever. So, our brains take that concept and adjust the speed in which it deletes and pushes back information, just not always the correct information.

Our moral compass is always at work, and always pointing in the direction we would like to believe we encompass. We want to make decisions that are objective of bias, logical in scope, and thorough with the information that has been given. When we are distracted, overwhelmed, anxious, or inattentive, those biases that we try so hard to push out, creep in a little at a time. Almost always, you are not conscious of those biases when you reach a decision about something. So, they are left in your decision making models and end with unfruitful decisions and judgments not based in fact and objective truth. Ultimately, you are making bad decisions.

## Causes of Cognitive Bias

We have gone over the obvious causes of cognitive bias - attention and personal biases - but when you reach beyond those, there are four very common biases that can affect anyone in regards to making choices. These causes are universal across all types and sectors of mental modelling, and they affect cognitive bias even when attention and personal bias are not an issue. Let's take a look at these four common causes.

## An Overabundance of Information

If you look at the world as a whole and how long human beings have been on it collecting data and evolving information, it becomes quite clear that no one can know or even process all of it. An overabundance of information can come from the general view that there is just far too much information out there for us to process. While humans have a tendency to tell themselves that they can do anything they put their mind to, there are limitations.

Your senses are the collectors of information, taking in data by using sight, hearing, smell, taste, and touch. We are constantly inputting and outputting, just like the computers that we ourselves created. However, on top of that, we live in a very large place. We live in houses, neighbourhoods, towns, counties, states, countries, hemispheres, on a planet in the solar system, and in the universe. From there, we don't know. For all we know, we are just a speck of sand in an extended and twisted multiverse. The amount of knowledge within those spaces is astronomical. It is nearly impossible to believe that it could be picked up by one person.

In fact, even here on our own planet, deep in the ocean, far into the trenches of the rainforests, we are still discovering new species of plants and animals. It is obvious that even if we were capable of taking in the information from all of these places, we would undoubtedly miss some. This is a fault of sorts - an evolutionary blockage that we have - and we will pass it on to other humans and to the artificial intelligence that we surround ourselves with.

As humans, we have to come to the conclusion that we are okay with the fact that we will never be able to understand everything that is out there. Our species is not large enough to fully grasp the power of that type of knowledge, and our reach is currently far too short to even try. The overabundance of information is hardly ever a blessing, and it is too often a distraction from what we should be focusing on.

## Connecting the Dots

Once you have collected all of that data - that raw information that you are either given, taught, or already knew - you have to do something with it. We, as humans, with the great power of our brains compared to other species, process that information into meaningful data. In order to do that, we have to take two sides and figure out how to connect the dots between them. On one side, we have the limited raw data and information we collected, and on the other side, we have the numerous mental models, our personal beliefs, professional beliefs, symbols, biases, and associations from when the situation had found us in the past.

When you connect the dots, you are often doing it without any information to back you up. You will connect them together in the best way possible by using your preconceived ideas, history, and personal convictions as the thread. When you are through, you have this mental model created from your own brain that is a combination of new information and old information. These new stories or decisions are based off of the fact that you began to tether the ideas together the best you could. In reality, though, these new ideas will be seething with past information. They will not be clear and concise.

## Time Is of the Essence

Time seems to be a constant theme in our lives. When we are young, we can't wait for time to go by, wanting to become adults, have jobs, and be someone of importance. Then when we reach the lacklustre reality of it all, and we wish for time to speed up so we can get to retirement to enjoy our older years like we so richly deserve. However, somewhere in there, between the meetings and the marriage, the children and the corporate meetings, we realize that time is actually finite.

There is no real difference when it comes to decisions. No matter what model we use, no one, not even a computer, could sit and go through every single option for the issue at hand. While some things might seem like they are cut and dry, statistically speaking, that is not the case. It would take multiple lifetimes just to decide what you wanted for breakfast if you had to think of every option out there. Considering your life is a pretty important resource that would run out long before you actually finished looking at the choices - and you'd be pretty hungry.

## Human RAM

So, for argument's sake, let's assume that you could take in all the information out there on your subject, you could turn and process it into meaningful, bias-lacking, information, and you had super speed when you did it. There is still one really huge problem - our brains do not have the space to hold all the information, all our symbolism, all our stories, and all of our past choices. Our brains know that there is limited space in there, and that, ultimately, it has to let some things go in order to keep the important information there.

Am I saying this is why we constantly lose our keys? No, but if you have a very mentally demanding job, that could play a part. If the information is small, and it clears up space for what you are working on it that moment, your brain will kick it to the curb - or at least store it in that subconscious so when you go looking for them, it drives you crazy because you know you know where you put them, but you just can't pull that memory.

Oftentimes, a way we pull in more information when our brains are bulging is by generalizing the facts, identifying patterns within the data so we don't have to remember every word, and by trying to compartmentalize everything in there. However, if you do that, aren't you basically defeating the purpose of pulling all that information in the first place? Now you've dumbed it down without knowing if you'll be able to retrieve it when you need to. While it seems we made computers in our image (minus the emotional stuff), they aren't super-bots either. They only have a certain amount of storage space, and sometimes, it'll start deleting if you don't keep up with it.

Now, because both cognitive bias and logical fallacies can come into play in mental models, let's clear up what the two are and how they are different.

## Cognitive Bias vs. Logical Fallacy

Seeing as we now know all about cognitive bias, we should begin to understand its buddy, logical fallacy. They are not the same. Many psychologists and philosophers have debated the differences between the two, but in the end, both have a very distinct definition. At the same time, one can also be malicious in nature.

A logical fallacy is a common error in reason that undermines the logic and truth of your argument. These fallacies can fall in line with illegitimate arguments and ones that don't even closely resemble the issue being talked about. They can also spew their point of view but have absolutely no evidence or completely biased evidence to back them up. It seems that in this day and age of tumultuous politics, people find themselves battling back and forth, having negative information thrown at them without any type of explanation or proof. Most of the time, it's personal emotion mixed with media bias. Either way, it's not a good combination.

Looking at cognitive bias, which is a falsity in logic due to underlying experiences, attention, and many other things, it is not intentional. Logical fallacies are known to be somewhat intentional and often malicious. Below we have detailed some different types of logical fallacies to look out for.

**1. Slippery slope-** A slippery slope fallacy is best described as a hasty conclusion where someone equates an idea by skipping the steps in between to a final conclusion that could be a thousand steps away.

*Example: If we make a law that prohibits smoking on government property, then the government will ban cigarettes all together, making it illegal to smoke anywhere at any time.*

In this example, they jumped from a logical event to the worst case scenario, skipping all steps that would need to occur for landing at the end without cause.

**2. Hasty generalization-** A hasty generalization is reaching an ultimate conclusion based on your own personal bias and without fact or evidence to back it up.

*Example: Even though I've never met Sally, I can tell by her picture at the beach I won't like her.*

In this example, they prejudged Sally with personal bias without any evidence to back up their claim. Oftentimes, hasty generalization can lead to a missed opportunity, because you will put a negative thought on an opportunity before even giving it a chance.

**3. Post hoc ergo propter hoc:** This is a decision or conclusion decided upon by assuming that if the first situation occurred after the second, then the second must have caused the first.

*Example: I drank a bottle of soda, and now I have indigestion, so the soda must have caused it.*

In this example, they are blaming the soda for indigestion without sufficient proof. Indigestion could have come from a number of things, but they have equated the first situation with the second.

**4. Genetic fallacy-** A genetic fallacy can be really bad at times. It is the belief that the origin of a person, an idea, an institute, or a theory determines the character, nature, or worth of that person, place, or thing.

*Example: The news article is a conservative publication, so you know whatever they print has to be true.*

In this example, they believed that because the publication shared their ideals, everything they printed was absolutely true. This goes against facts and logic.

**5. Circular argument-** A circular argument is simply restating a claim instead of giving any back-up or factual evidence. They ignore any question being asked.

*Example: You should invite your aunt to the wedding because it would be mean to not invite her.*

In this example, the person basically said the same thing in two different ways.

**6. Either/or-** This type of logical fallacy over-simplifies a conversation by giving only two options (usually the best and the worst).

*Example: We either go on a diet or die from obesity.*

In this example, the person gave an ultimatum, basically. They completely left out the millions of other choices that sit between the two theories.

**7. Ad hominem-** An ad hominem is when, instead of giving their facts and evidence for a statement, a person hurls attacks at others.

*Example: Vegans struggle to get people on board with their cause because they are loud, obnoxious, and dirty hippies.*

In this example, they began the sentence by stating their concern or their topic of discussion but ended it with an attack instead of saying why they thought Vegans were struggling.

**8. Bandwagon-** The bandwagon fallacy is when a group mentality is pushed onto a person in order to get them to believe what they believe.

*Example: If you truly believed in this country, you would let everyone, including children, own machine guns.*

In this example, the person is using the country as a whole group to get the other to believe in allowing children and citizens of the country to own machine guns.

**9. Red herring-** This is one of politics' greatest fallacies. Not only do politicians use it, but the supporters do as well. With so many issues being faced, it's hard not to accidentally slip into this fallacy on a regular basis.

*Example: I think what she wore is inappropriate, and the other party couldn't stop talking about my friend when they didn't like what she wore.*

In this example, instead of stating why they thought what she wore was inappropriate, they threw in a situation that was unrelated in an attempt to show cause, but not toward the initial person. They were dodging the original portion by stating something emotional afterward.

**10. Moral equivalence-** A moral equivalence is when minor infractions are compared to major ones, basically insinuating that they are both equally as immoral.

*Example: Anyone who supports gun rights hates children.*

At the beginning, this example shows the topic of contention but then skips over to a completely ridiculous statement trying to draw a rise out of the other person.

These are just some logical fallacies, and the list seems to grow on a daily basis. Now that we understand these, let's sink back into cognizant bias for a bit to understand the different types and how they affect mental modelling.

# Chapter 8
# Applying Creativity to Improve your Life

Are you one of those people that have completely given up on creativity? There are a lot of people like this, never seeing creativity as a way to improve their lives in any way. Many see creativity as hobby-orientated and never think to apply it to any situation where a solution is required. There isn't one answer to every situation, there are many, and using creativity opens up a whole new world, bringing tons of benefits with it.

Some people mistakenly see creativity as an obstinate attitude and they feel that, when others insist on doing something in a different way, this indicates that they are stubborn. In fact, creative people have more ideas, better ideas and better solutions to a situation than anyone who doesn't use the creative part of their brain.

Don't hold good ideas back

We are all different and we are all free to see things in any way we choose, in our own unique ways. Any way that you interpret a situation is creativity at work and, when you use that creativity to its best, you will find that you can come up with loads of different and innovative solutions for times when you need a quick answer.

Do you remember a TV show called MacGyver? He was a very creative character, using anything that came to hand to get himself out of a tight situation and that is something that anyone of us can do.

## You Never Stop Learning Creativity

Whatever you experience in life, you will learn something from it and you will gain benefits from it. Those benefits can be put to good use later on in life, when you face real situations that need a solution. Being creative means that you may have to think outside the box on occasion, and allow your mind to venture into previously untouched territory. Creative people can never be certain how their ideas are going to pan out, until they actually put those ideas into practice and, to be fair, where creativity is concerned, provided the idea is a safe one then you have nothing to lose.

## Why Should You Be Creative?

When you have to find a new solution or adapt a current one to fit new circumstances, the purpose of it is to improve what's already there or, to put it more simply, make things better! That's what creativity is all about; coming up with solutions that please everyone and that make the situation better for everyone as well.

## 16 Qualities That Creative Thinkers Have

There's an old saying – "the more you do of what you are doing, the more you will get of what you've got." When it comes to creative thinking, you must keep on digging deeper inside of yourself to come up with bigger and better ideas to improve your life. Creative thinkers tend to possess 16 qualities and when you use at least one, preferably more, of those qualities, you start to think of yourself as a genius. Those 16 qualities are:

- They keep asking questions

Creative thinkers tend to be highly curious people and will constantly be asking questions – why, why not, why can't we do it that way? So what if we've never done it that way before, we can try it now can't we? Because of the question, it makes other people look at things differently as well.

- They practice zero-based thinking

What is zero-based thinking? The easiest way to answer that is in a question. Creative thinkers continually ask themselves "if I wasn't doing what I'm doing now, knowing what I know now, would I start the job again?" And, guess what, if the answer is no, they simply stop what they are doing. Ask yourself the same question next time you are doing something – you might be surprised at what the answer is. It's astonishing how many people continue doing something even though they know, deep down, that they should not have even started the job. And then they wonder why they aren't getting very far!

- They are prepared to change their minds

Creative thinkers are very willing to change their minds about something. In this day and age, a willingness to change is a death knell and creative thinkers would rather have their destiny in their own hands, rather than in someone else's. And they prefer to make the decision on when to change, rather than get caught up in a flood when change is inevitable. That way, they are prepared and they stay one step ahead. A truly creative thinker, a flexible thinker will say just four words – "I changed my mind." It's as simple as that. Research has shown that an alarming 70% of the decisions that we make turn out to be wrong and a willingness to change your mind is vital for the good of your life in the long run. To be successful in today's world you must be mentally flexible.

- They can admit when they are wrong

Being able to admit when you are wrong about something is not a sign of weakness. Look at it this way – when you know that you have made a wrong decision but don't want to admit it, do you find yourself getting exhausted? Suffering from brain fog? But you persist anyway. Did you know that, by not admitting that you are wrong, by continuing to push on despite that fact, you will burn up virtually all of your emotional and mental energy? Creative thinkers are open-minded, they are flexible and fluid. As well as being able to change their minds easily, they can also admit that they made a mistake.

- They continue to learn

People who are very creative can easily say, "I don't know." They know that we can't possibly know everything there is to know about everything and that it's highly likely they could be wrong about something. If they are asked a question and they really don't know the answer, they will say so. They won't waffle or spout some rubbish to try and hide their ignorance. Instead, they will go off and find the answer. Think about this important point – if you are struggling with something, there is an extremely high chance that, somewhere in the world, somewhere in time, someone else has had the same problem and they will have solved it. The most creative thing you can do is to find that person or that answer and use it. The person who is the smartest isn't necessarily the person who came up with the solution – that could have been just pure luck. The smartest people are those who go find that answer and then use it.

- They are goal-oriented

Creative thinkers always have a goal in mind. They know what they want, have probably even written it down, very clearly, step by step. They see it in their minds eye every day. They like to imagine their goal, to see it as if it were a reality. And, the more they do this, the more creative they get and the more likely they are to achieve that goal.

- Their egos are not so involved

When a creative thinker is proved right, there is no real involvement of the ego. They don't care who is right, they care what is right and they will willingly accept ideas and help from anyone or any source to achieve their goals.

- They always change the things around them

Creative thinkers are the kind of people who always like to keep things different. They rarely get satisfied with something so much as to keep them the same way for a very long period of time. More than that, creative thinkers are aware that if they stay focused or become stagnant on one thing for far too long, they might lose their creative spark – something they would never risk doing.

- They are in a never-ending hunt for new experiences

While other people accept opportunities when they come knocking at their doors, creative thinkers go out, look for those opportunities, and chase them. They are the kind of people who are always looking for new experiences because they need something to trigger or stimulate their creativity. They need new and exciting experiences that can give them a certain adrenaline rush or a "Eureka!" moment. Otherwise, their creativity will be unused and will stagnate. Getting out there and having new experiences is a perfect way to broaden one's horizons and acquire creative inspiration.

- They are very keen observers

Creative thinkers observe people as well as situations. Creative thinkers are people who are naturally curious. At any given place and time, various things are happening all around them, and creative thinkers always make use of this opportunity to observe everything of anything – from the smallest details to the biggest ones. They also make sure to people-watch and spend time observing the different kinds of people around them. This quality allows creative thinkers to expand their horizons as well and discover something new. They put the observations they experience aside for later use as these could also enable them to gain a better appreciation of the things and the people around them – something creative thinkers could use so as to come up with an idea that possibly takes in the perspective of others or an idea which could help those they have observed. In this way, they are empathetic.

- They look at life in a very positive way

Creative thinkers view life in two levels: (1) a continuous journey of self-expression; and (2) a big roller coaster ride with so many challenges they can build on and learn from. Creative thinkers, you could say, are optimists. They look at life and see a huge arena for them to express themselves. They fully believe that life should be referred to as a piece of art wherein all people would have to do is to let their creativity flow and do things that would show the entire world who they really are. More than that, creative thinkers do not get knocked down by the challenges that life brings. They understand that everyone goes through life and experiences all kinds of pain, but they know that how people respond to these pains is completely up to them. Creative thinkers respond to these hardships by turning all the negative emotions and feelings into something beautiful that people can relate to.

- They "get in the zone"

Have you ever experienced writing, singing, dancing, painting or doing any creative activity of some sort and completely drown out the world around you? Creative thinkers are always prone to this. When they begin doing something that tickles the creative part of their brains, they eventually get lost in it and "get in the zone." It's like nothing else matters and it's just them and their paintbrush or microphone, pen or music. They just become so invested and so focused on the activity because they do it with so much passion and with every fiber of their being. This goes well with the theory that multi-taskers are actually doing themselves a disservice because they cannot give everything that they have to multiple tasks at a time.

- They are big on daydreaming

While most people see daydreaming as a way for people to relax and slack off, creative thinkers know that there's more to daydreaming than that. Daydreaming, for them, is one of the greatest tools they can use to nurture and develop their ideas. They let their minds run free and imagine all kinds of things that they can make happen in real life. Daydreaming in itself is also a big booster of creativity because it triggers our brains to become imaginative and exhaust our creative potentials.

- They know how and when to make the most of their time

Creative thinkers know exactly when they are most productive and make the most of that time. Whether it's in the morning, evening, or somewhere in the middle, creative thinkers are aware that it's essential for them to make use of their productive period to come up with a brand new creative idea and work on it.

- They are risk-takers

Creative thinking alone already involves numerous risks. The mere idea of being unsure whether the product will be finished or if it will be of good quality the moment it's finished but doing them anyway are risks that creative thinkers take every day. Taking risks will enable creative thinkers to gain more ideas as well as to grow their own creativity. Taking risks of any kind gives people the chance to discover and try something they've never tried before – which is heaven for their creative juices.

- They give themselves an "alone time"

Although creative thinkers like to be with people in general, they also know when they need to have time to themselves and "let the dust settle" so to speak. This alone time allows creative thinkers to let their minds wander off away from any form of distraction that could impede their creativity. They also use this time to work and get things done.

Upon knowing these 16 qualities that more often than not describe creative thinkers, it's now time for you to check yourself in the mirror to see whether you're up to the creative challenge.

## Being Creative Means You Have More Ideas

This is so true. If you have a creative mind, you will find that you can generate more ideas, without even really trying. And, the more idea you come up with, the better the quality of those ideas. With so many ideas, there is also a high probability of you coming up with the right idea when it's needed. Do you remember this famous quote by Thomas Edison – "Genius is 1% inspiration and 99% perspiration"?

He was dead right. Coming up with the idea takes about 1% of the total equation. A real mark of genius is your ability to generate the idea, test it, and make sure it works and then implement and execute it in your own life to get the result you want. When you have an idea write it down. Plan the way you are going to implement it in your life, through creative thinking, and then do it. The more you use your creativity in this manner, the more you are going to achieve.

# Chapter 9
# Improve Your Mental Models

With the recent prominence of the cognitive behavioural sciences comes the rise of mental models as well. There are literally thousands of them now, but they are also not created equally. The mental models you currently hold are not the best for the goal in life that you want to achieve.

Identifying the mental models that you need to have can be a daunting task, given the multitude of options you have on your hands. To help you through this process, here are four mental models derived from different fields of interest that you may be able to apply into life and improve the way you think, decide, and act.

## Mental Model in Economics: Gresham's Law

The principle of bad elements driving out the good elements from a system over time is what constitutes Gresham's Law.

## Historical Background

As a financier during the Tudor reign in England, Sir Thomas Gresham explained that forged coins could replace the real coins as the instigators of forgery hoarded the latter and let the rest of the population use the fake currency for transactions. Without any form of verification or checkpoints, no one but the culprits could immediately recognize the differences between the two types of coins.

The exact origin of this mental model, however, is contested by experts on cognitive science and mental models. Some believe that the concept behind Gresham's Law has been proposed earlier by Nicolaus Copernicus around forty years before Sir Thomas Gresham did. The latter only managed to be more successful in drawing the attention of more people into the existence of the problems caused by a bad coinage. As such, selected literature about this mental model refers to the principle as the Gresham-Copernicus' Law.

Still, there are researchers who believe that the earliest record of this issue about the circulation of fake currency is from Aristophanes, a playwright from ancient Greece. One of his plays highlights the similarities between the decay of great politicians with the introduction of bad coins into society.

In the modern days, the problem with fake currency has mostly been effectively addressed by banks and financial institutions. However, the problems that this situation causes remain significant enough to merit the legacy of Gresham's Law. The conclusion of Aristophanes' play is reflected in the way humans succumb to the pressures of their peers and society as a whole. If a person adopts a destructive behaviour, it is almost impossible to drive out that behaviour as long as the person believes that he or she gets some sort of survival advantage or benefit out of the said behaviour. In this way, Gresham's Law bears similarities with the principle of evolution by natural selection—wherein organisms that possess qualities that allow them to survive live on, while those that don't die out.

## Gresham's Law in Action

The general rule is that if a behaviour serves a practical and competitive purpose, it will take root and continue to be carried out until it has outlived its usefulness or until another superior behaviour replaces it. Because of these organizations and individuals who are only interested in their betterment and interests are more likely to fall under the effects described by Gresham's Law. The only way to circumvent this is to establish control points and maintain a check-and-balance system. Otherwise, the bad but beneficial practices would drive out morality and ethics until the organization or individual has become fully corrupted.

For you to better visualize the effects of this principle, here are some sample scenarios on how bad could drive the good out of a system:

1. Anna and Rachel are competing for medical technicians who work for the same company by selling a particular brand of anti-depressants.

Anna employs bribery as one of her primary strategies for making a sale. Though she has several tools under her belt that would help her convince doctors to choose her product, she has observed that bribing them is the most effective and efficient method. As such, she has no qualms about bribing doctors left and right just to reach her monthly sales target.

On the other hand, Rachel refuses to succumb to unethical practices of selling her product. She relies on her training as a salesperson and the network she has built over the years. Because of this, there are times where she struggles to meet the sales target, stressing her and her team leader as a result.

If the medical industry itself does not punish fraudulent selling tactics, and the company continues to prioritize profits over ethical business practices, Anna would continue to maintain a sustainable advantage over Rachel. This advantage would further strengthen Anna's bad behaviour since she will be rewarded with bonuses and promotions.

Over time, even if checkpoints become established in the system, Anna is not likely going to change her tactics. Instead, she would actively look for ways to continue bribing her way into selling anti-depressants to willing doctors.

2. During the 2008 financial crisis in the US stock market, experts believe that one of the causes of this meltdown is the sub-prime lending practices of institutions that provide mortgage lending services. Banks have always competed amongst each other over which one of them would be able to attract the number of borrowers. To protect themselves and the market itself, systems and standards are put into place. However, in the process of gaining an advantage over the others, a significant number of banks had allowed their standards to slide down to zero.

Failing to realize that it would become a losing endeavour in the future, both the lenders and borrowers succumb to the short-term benefits and incentives of sub-par lending practices. Banks allowed less stringent verification of loan applicants, while borrowers become encouraged by the promise of flexible and more manageable interest rates. In the end, due to the disregard for the proven lending and borrowing system, the market crashed—causing the closure of several financial institutions and significant losses for the borrowers.

3. Mackenzie King, a former Canadian prime minister, discusses the similarities of Gresham's Law and the Law of Competition, leading him to call the combined

effects of both on the market as the "Law of Competing Standard".

According to him, the competing standards within the same industry become imbalanced when some companies choose to do underhanded methods to lower their costs, thereby making their commodities or services more attractive to consumers. This can take various forms of unethical practices, such as illegally outsourcing labour into third-world countries, using sub-standard or even harmful materials, or padding products with unnecessary fillers.

Much like Gresham's observations about the disappearance of precious metals, the well-meaning intentions of companies to provide products and services that would be useful or helpful to the consumers would eventually become less of a priority to the industry. Instead, material gain would take precedence over quality and good customer service. Consumers might not realize at first the effect of this transition to the worse; Therefore, they would unwittingly strengthen the bad practices of the companies that offer cheaper commodities or services.

Prime Minister King then concluded that to prevent this from happening, high standards must be established as a basis for the checkpoints that will be applied by the industry to its players. Though it may be hard, he implored the different government agencies and private institutions to aid him in providing a guarantee of value for money to the consumers in general.

## How Gresham's Law Can Improve Your Mental Models

Taking into account the phenomenon described by Gresham's Law, one could say that the best way to prevent the establishment of weak or destructive mental models is to put into place checkpoints on your own behaviour. Employ a personal check-and-balance system to identify immediately bad practices and then recognize them for what they really are. They might benefit you in the short-term, but over time, continuing such bad practices could physically, emotionally, or mentally corrupt you.

In the event that the bad practice has already been ingrained in your system, the best way to handle such cases is to remove yourself from a permitting environment. Look for a more controlling environment that could keep you in line despite the urge to succumb to your impulses.

Without the chance to experience the supposed benefits of the bad practice, you would eventually realize that the negative effects of doing so overpowers whatever advantage you gain from it. Over time, the lack of opportunity to practice would also allow you to phase it out of your system and hopefully replace it with better and more ethical behaviours.

## Mental Model in Systems: Pareto's Principle

Essentially, Pareto's Principle describes one of the so-called "universal truths" that 80% of the total output comes only from 20% of the input.

## Historical Background

In the late 19th century, economist/philosopher from Italy V. F. Damaso Pareto first proposed his theory that 80% of the total results from only 20% of the actions done for a given activity. This idea stems initially while he was out in the garden. As he was taking note of his harvest at that time, he realized that from the pea plants in the garden, only about 20% produced almost 80% of high-quality pea pods that he has harvested. This discovery led him to wonder if this imbalance of inputs and outputs also applies to other areas. To do this, he focused first on the obviously uneven wealth distribution in their country at the time. Upon examining the records of land ownership, he found out that from the aggregate population, only 20% owned 80% of all the lands that can be owned by private citizens. Furthermore, he realized that only a vital few — the top 20% of the population — holds the power over the trivial many, or the bottom 80% of the country's population.

Searching for more proof, he turned his focus towards the different industries. He was pleased to learn that his theory continued to hold up. According to the data he has gathered, 80% of the total production for a given industry was generated by only 20% of the companies within that said industry. This observation remains consistent across various fields, so he concluded that his theory could be considered a generality.

## Pareto's Principle in Action

Pareto's Principle is one of the most widely known concepts in business and economics. While the ratio is not always exactly 80:20, the logic behind this imbalance stands firm across different situations. For example:

- In the field of sales and marketing, only 20% of the total number of agents manage to generate 80% of the gross sales for a given period.

- A catering company observed that 80% of its profits come from only 20% of the clients they have handled.

- Software engineers of a particular word processing app noted that 20% of the reported software bugs have caused nearly 80% of the crashes of their software.

- The Department of Health reviewed its statistical data for a given year and discovered that 80% of the total spending on healthcare can be accounted to only 20% of the total population.

- Business executives have also noted the importance of applying the Pareto Principe in overcoming the challenges of having limited resources. Given the scope of their responsibilities, they do not only have to manage their own time but also of their respective teams. Rather than aim for the impossible, the Pareto Principle allows them to figure out the priorities that would give them the most results. As for the rest of their probable goals, they could just put them aside for the time being, or even discard them completely.

- Many freelancers are using this principle sometimes without even realizing it. Since not all freelancers are fortunate enough to have a steady stream of work, they have to smart about choosing their clients. Aside from financial gains, it is also important for them to select only a few, but well-paying clients because having too many bosses at a given time can increase the likelihood of being burnt out.

- Given their nature, entrepreneurs are always tempted to go after and push through business ideas that may or may not pan out. To avoid wasting time and capital, some entrepreneurs apply this principle in order to determine whether or not a business is worth pursuing. After all, it is perfectly alright to take calculated risks, especially in business. However, this does not mean that they would have to witness all their efforts to go down the drain just because they do not know when to keep fighting and when to call it off.

## How Pareto's Principle Can Improve Your Mental Models

The Pareto Principle can be applied to any situation, including your course to personal improvement. Learning which of your tasks and activities are essential to your success is a great way of putting direction and speed into this endeavour. Many experts also recommend the application of Pareto Principle into one's goal-setting exercises. Rather than simply making a list of the things you want to achieve, analyze the list further by identifying which of them should be your priority. By doing so, you are assured that you would get significant results, while still having some time left to do the other periphery goals in your list.

The Pareto Principle can also be of aid to those who have the tendency to procrastinate, especially at work. Many people tend to put off big tasks in favour of small doable tasks, thinking that these small steps would build and grow into something significant. However, studies show that doing the most complex tasks that comprise 20% of your list could give you tremendous rewards that you would not have gotten otherwise. Furthermore, if you develop a habit of doing only small, low-value tasks, you would eventually find it hard to complete the important, high-value activities that you should have prioritized in the first place.

## Mental Model in Biology: Evolution by Natural Selection

### Historical Background

The concept of evolution has long been introduced before Charles Darwin and his fateful voyage to Madagascar. What elevates the theory of Darwin is the evolutionary mechanism called natural selection. Through this, he was able to explain how certain organisms manage to adapt better with their respective environments compared to the others.

Darwin reached his concept of natural selection through the following key observations:

- Most traits can be passed by the parent organism to its offspring.

- Offspring are often produced beyond the number that can be reasonably sustained by their environment. As a result, competition arises over the limited resources available.

- Offspring that belong to the same generation vary from one another depending on the traits each has inherited from the parent.

- From these observations, Darwin arrived at the following conclusions:

  o Within a given population, certain organisms would inherit key traits that would make them more effective in terms of survival and reproduction compared to the other organisms of the same species who did not receive the same set of traits.

- o Because organisms with the helpful traits produce more offspring, and because these helpful traits are heritable, there will be more organisms bearing these helpful traits, thus making the traits more common within their generation.

- o As time goes by, succeeding generations would be able to better adapt to the environment, making them more successful than their parents were at survival and reproduction.

The model of evolution that Darwin developed allowed him to make sense of the patterns that he had observed during his trip. For example, different species of Galapagos finches share certain traits because they also share the same ancestors. However, if a certain group of organisms became isolated from the rest for several generations, that particular group develops a distinct set of traits that allowed them to survive and thrive in the environment of the island where they can be found. As a result, beaks of different shapes and sizes can be observed among the distinct species of finches that live in different islands of Madagascar.

Over the course of multiple studies conducted on Darwin's theory, experts on this mental model have managed to boil down its prerequisites into the following:

1. Replication - The ability to create new copies with a high level of fidelity with the immediate source

2. Mutation - The ability of the said copies to change in a slight, but potentially significant ways

3. Fitness - Copies should be able to persist and reproduce at various rates

When all three elements are present, you can expect the copies to survive and multiply with a high level of success. Copies that lack any of the given elements are likely going to die off, eventually.

## Evolution by Natural Selection in Action

Over the years, Darwin's model of evolution by natural selection has gained popularity and massive support from the different communities. It should be noted, however, that not everything is capable of undergoing this process of evolution. To better understand this concept, there are some common answers of people when asked about the things that can evolve:

1. As evidenced by archaeological findings, homo sapiens has beat out other species, including Neanderthals and apes, among others. Believing that this is an evidence of evolution, however, is inaccurate. Following the three elements required for something to evolve, replication is absent in this particular case. You might counter this by saying that humans replicate themselves by mating and

producing children. Again, this is false because parents do not reproduce high-fidelity versions of themselves. The children will inherit certain traits from the mother and the father, but they will never be nearly exact copies of one or the other.

The correct answer, in this case, is that the human genes evolve. These are the building blocks of human evolution. Genes can replicate themselves over and over—with a small likelihood of undergoing mutation in the process.

2. Biological evolution is often the foremost example that comes to mind for most people. However, when analyzed carefully, cultural evolution also undergoes natural selection. First proposed by Joseph Henrich, the idea that human culture also evolves following similar patterns as genes do seem implausible. Upon closer examination, however, the three elements of evolution by natural selection are present whenever there is a shift in human culture.

In terms of replication, humans are natural at mimicking the behaviours of others, even without fully understanding the rationale behind the said action. By studying the ways of the people, they admire or respect, people are able to replicate with high fidelity certain aspects of other people's behaviours. Mutation plays a part because even though humans have high levels of skill when it comes to copying others, it is impossible to be perfect at all times. There are also instances where the initial copy is already wrong in some way, so when it gets replicated, the imperfection is passed on to more people.

The fitness of cultural behaviours is evident because humans only tend to mimic behaviours that they find beneficial or pleasing. Otherwise, the behaviour will eventually die down until no one else would ever remember how to do it and why it was done in the first place.

Given these, one can argue that cultural practices are evolving by natural selection. A group's language, rituals, religions, and special tools are all part of the culture, and can, therefore, evolve as they get passed on to the younger generation.

## How Evolution by Natural Selection Can Improve Your Mental Models

There are various ways on how you can apply the principles of evolution by natural selection into your day-to-day life. First, you may be able to better assess the likelihood of success and longevity of the system you are creating by examining it against the core tenets of evolution by natural selection. Does your system provide opportunities for faithful replication? Is there an allowance for positive mutation? Does it exhibit signs of fitness? Answering yes to all of these questions is a good indicator that you are on the right track.

The concepts that define evolution by natural selection can also improve the way you solve problems. Rather than rely solely on logic, you may also come up with various approaches, mutate each one in slightly different ways, replicate, and then keep only the one that would work best.

# Chapter 10
# Mental Toughness Training in Setting Goals

Mental toughness. Google these words, and you will find millions of hits with anecdotes about Olympic athletes, West Point graduates, and military personnel. You will also find stories of how people just like you used this high-class skill to reach new heights in their own lives.

Mental toughness is the key skill that makes the difference between a benched high school baseball pitcher going pro and never playing again. It's the difference between the Etsy shop that just kind of peters out and one that becomes the owner's full living. It's the difference between your stagnancy and your glowing future. Another, simpler word for mental toughness that you've probably heard before is this: grit.

Determination. Perseverance. More than intelligence or genes or talent, this is the stuff that's been shown to set successful people apart from the rest. It's the drive to achieve long-term goals, even when it's tough, or you don't feel like it. Even when roadblocks rise up to defeat you, with grit, you won't back down.

At the very core of mental toughness is consistency. Once you create a goal, consistently striving toward it every day, one step at a time, is what's going to earn you grit. If you're an artist or want to be, that looks like creating something, even if it's small, every single day without failing. If you're an athlete, it looks like showing up early to practice every single time, completely focused and ready to go, and never missing a workout. If you're a nurse, it looks like showing up for your patients, even when you're tired, in any form they need you to be.

The great news about mental toughness is this: you can have it. That voice in your head, that's been telling you someone else deserves your dreams because they're just more talented or have better skills than you, is wrong. Talent and genetics can be completely overrun by one person who has the drive and the willpower to focus hard on getting where they want to be. Anyone can achieve mental toughness. That anyone includes you.

Being mentally tough means, you'll be better prepared for change. It means you'll be more positive under pressure, more productive during the workday, and harness more emotional stability. It means you'll grow into the part of yourself that believes your happiness has nothing to do with your external world and everything to do with your internal world.

Being mentally tough means, you'll focus on your goals and dreams instead of just reacting to life as it comes. You'll be more patient with the outcomes because you can see clearly how you're getting there, and you'll experience a more relaxed, content countenance. All of this can be yours. Are you ready to begin?

## Training Yourself to be Mentally Tough

### <u>Step One: Know What You Want</u>

To start with, you have to know what you want. You have to be able to picture it clearly in your mind. The first step is to make a clear, attainable goal. Define what being mentally tough looks like in context for you.

If you want to clean up your finances, maybe your mental toughness training for the week is making dinner every night instead of succumbing to ordering takeout. If your goal is to be more knowledgeable this year, commit to reading a book a week for the rest of the year. If you want to work on sharpening your self-discipline skills, work your schedule so you can fit in a good habit, like meditating or jogging. If you've been really bad lately about being present in your relationships, maybe your first step is deciding to leave your phone somewhere out of sight and spend half an hour with your spouse and your kids.

Notice how none of these tasks seem to be mountains you couldn't climb. The task itself doesn't have to be gigantic. The hard part is doing it consistently, every day, working at it even when you don't want to. There will be days you don't feel like cooking. Grit is grown by doing it when the motivation is at an all-time low, just because you know you should.

When creating these goals, keep in mind where your roadblocks will be. Make sure the tasks you create to accomplish your goals are built into your routine to become a habit. When you don't want to or don't feel like showing up, accomplishing your task out of habit will save you. Remember that being mentally tough isn't about what feels good. It's about sticking to the schedule regardless of how you feel about it. It's about being consistent with your habits and your routine to get to your goal. That's what's going to set you apart. Every day when you complete your task, be sure to celebrate your progress and your wins. Every step you take is getting you closer to the person you want to be.

## Step Two: Tweak Your Self-Talk

Your brain is a powerful machine, and it's constantly working. Whether you realize it or not, you say 300 to 1,000 words per minute to yourself. What do they sound like? It might not seem like a big deal when you mutter, "Oh, that was stupid," to yourself after making a mistake, or, "Yikes, that could've gone better," when you bomb a presentation. But for Navy SEALs, self-talk can mean the difference between passing or failing. Welcome to the Pool Comp.

The Pool Competency Test is all about staying calm and positive when everything around you threatens danger. Imagine this: you're underwater, decked out in scuba gear. Everything is normal, in the surreal kind of way the world feels underwater. Suddenly, the equipment feeding oxygen to your mouth is ripped out, and the tube filling oxygen to that mouthpiece is tied in a knot.

If we went into this exercise cold-turkey, without any training, our hearts would be racing. This is a matter of life and death. You have to get your equipment back under control. But your hands are shaking, your mind is racing, and your heart rate won't relax for an instant. Panic sets in. Game over.

While our challenges might not be pool competency tests, this is a great example of how training your mind to be tough can affect how you behave, react, and get after your goals. The SEALs who were able to think rationally and positively about their outcomes while their lives were at stake were the ones who passed the exam, and also the ones who have the greatest mental toughness.

Outside of possibly saving your life, studies show that being positive is actually beneficial in many ways. Gratitude is proven to cause an increase in happiness, which is no surprise, considering gratitude is a self-discipline that makes us see the world around us positively.

Positivity can also be infectious in your relationships. A term called social optimism states that merely believing that people will like you will actually make people like you more. Optimism can benefit you at work by creating more opportunities for you, just because your positive mindset is sure you can achieve them.

Tweaking your self-talk towards positivity sounds easy and straight-forward enough, but so many of us have negative self-talk already programmed into our brains as a habit. You have to rewire yourself to think positively. Start by coming up with truthful affirmations for moments of panic and anxiety. Pessimism tends to tell you that bad things last forever, are universal, and mean you're a horrible person. Here's an example.

Another candidate gets the job you've been working for the past year to earn. Pessimism tells you this bad thing will last forever. Your mind might say, "I'm never going to leave this office." Instead, tell yourself the truth: bad things pass. "I am going to get a better position. It's just not happening this time."

Similarly, pessimism will tell you that bad things are universal. You walk out to the parking lot of the grocery store and find that your car's been hit, just in time to watch a teenager peel out of the parking lot and onto the adjacent street.

Fuming, you're probably thinking, "This would happen to me today! Things like this always happen to me!" Instead of digging yourself into a rut of self-pity, change your thoughts. Bad things have specific causes and don't just happen to you. Bad things are not universal.

The last place your mind tends to wander when it's in danger is to blame yourself. You finally got that new job you've been gunning for, but it's really difficult. Even in training, your new position requires a lot of concentration and study to understand. Everything is unfamiliar. You might trudge home thinking, "I'm worthless. I can't do this." But is that the truth? No. The truth is that you're struggling with a new skill. You are not terrible at this job just because you're struggling with it.

Another tool to battle pessimism is to argue with yourself. If your brain is telling you something negative, use a mental model like Elon Musk's First Principles to dig to the root of the negativity. If the thought is, "I'll never be a good dad," question why you think that. Is it because you don't have much experience in childcare? Is it because you'd like to be different from your dad and you're not sure how to do that?

Come up with a logical counter-argument, based in fact instead of emotion (like your original negative thought probably is). Suddenly, "I'll never be a good dad," turns into, "I don't have much experience with children, but if I work at it, I can have good relationships with children." If you decide, your negative thought is one that needs to be countered even further, make it a point to create goals that will strengthen your counter-argument. Offer to babysit for your friends or a family member. Ask for help from a mom or a dad, and talk to them about your fears.

Often, positivity is a skill that's overlooked because it's seen as less-than. People think of being positive as a piece of fluff to fill another line on the "special skills" section on your resume. The ever-faster, better, and stronger working monologue that's been ground into our brains says that any tool you can't use physically isn't worth using.

The truth about positivity, however, is that it's something much greater than we give it credit for. Some people are naturally positive. It doesn't take much for them to see something beautiful in the wreckage. Others struggle with this skill. Either way, strengthening it does more benefit for your health, for your future work, and your relationships.

What you'll start to realize as you practice positivity is that it's infectious. People will start to notice that you are "the happy person" or "the bright-side person," and they'll flock to you. Bosses want positive people on their teams. Potential boyfriends and girlfriends want positive people to love and love them. Your friends will start to catch the drift and develop a more positive perspective, too. When you look up, your life looks up.

Another tangible practice you can use to think more positively is to keep a gratitude journal. If you've been in the realm of personal growth long, you've heard this one a million times. That's because it works. Writing down things you're glad to have actually trains your mind to look for things that make your life as good as it is.

The change is slight at first. You might not recognize it after the first day, or even the first week, but it's there. In the back of your mind when you're struggling with pessimism, a little grateful voice will remind you of something good.

You can almost feel yourself getting a little lighter every time you write another thing or another person you're thankful is around. For the million and first time, consider keeping track of the things you're grateful for. Maybe that can be your new habit.

To sum it up:

1. Know what you want. Set a goal that's clear and attainable. Create new habits that will lead you to these goals.

2. Tweak your self-talk. Don't underestimate the power of positivity (or the power of pessimism).

Next up, we'll talk about some habits that mentally tough people put in place in their lives. Maybe you'll find one or two you already adhere to, or maybe you'll a couple that need to make a home in your schedule.

## Habits of Mentally Tough People

1. They surround themselves with people who think differently than them (especially if those different thinkers remind them of someone they want to be like).

Being around people who have had different experiences, different upbringings, or different areas of competence is a lesson in getting out of your comfort zone. We like to be comfortable. We like to stay in the realm of confidence, where we can predict what will happen next, and what we will do when it happens.

Being around people who lead different kinds of lives than you will open your eyes to situations you wouldn't run into on your own path. We all have different stories, different beliefs, and different dreams, and hearing about someone else's may just expand your own or awaken a passion you didn't know you had.

2. They engage in simulations of situations that terrify them.

How would you feel if right now, without any warning, you received a phone call for your dream job, and all you had to do was an interview for it in the next two minutes? Are your hands sweating just thinking about it? Even more than death, the number-one fear in America is oral communication. Simply verbally communicating under pressure is enough to make most of the United States tremble.

If you're one of the millions, and you hate interviews, wouldn't you like to make that experience a little easier? Simulating that terrifying situation can help. Conducting mock-interviews with family members and friends can help you to rehearse well-thought answers to typical interview questions.

When your future boss asks what your worst working trait is, you won't fumble over your words or laugh nervously if you've been over it a few times. Consider simulating the experience a trial run. The more trial runs you rehearse of a situation that scares you, the more confident you will be in that situation (and the less it will scare you).

3. They prepare.

True story: once on my first day at a new job, I forgot one of my shoes. I was running late that morning and threw both my shoes and my jacket into the passenger seat and took off for the office at a scary speed. I peeled into the parking lot, grabbed the keys out of the ignition, and went to put on my shoes, only to realize that only one of them was lying on the passenger seat.

I began a mad search for his brother. It wasn't under the passenger seat. It wasn't in between the seat and the console. It wasn't in the backseat. I started the morning fifteen minutes late, after limping into the nearest store with one shoe on my foot to buy new shoes. Later that night, I found my shoe on the floor of the garage, where it must have slipped out of my ill-prepared hands and onto the concrete slab.

The moral of the story is this: if I had woken up ten minutes earlier that morning and thought through the challenges of the day and fully prepared myself mentally for them, I probably would've shown up with both shoes on.

Preparing for the challenges ahead, both mentally and physically, will make you feel more confident and organized, put you at ease, and lend you a clearer, less emotional mind. You'll probably be wearing two shoes, too.

4. They are creative.

You are less likely to freeze under pressure if you already practice being creative and adaptable in your day-to-day life. Planning is great and needs to happen to prepare you for situational outcomes, but there will always be a kink in the plan.

There will always be something that doesn't go as it should have. In those instances, you will have to be creative and flexible to work around them. Great mothers and nannies do this phenomenally.

The plan may be to go to the park. Mom or babysitter has the baby backpack chock-full of tools for the day ahead because they planned for it. However, children are bundles of joy and surprises, so when the unthinkable happens, and little Johnny jumps straight into the water fountain, the caretaker has to be creative. Because she planned for the unexpected, she has an extra set of clothes for little Johnny.

However, when he then rolls around in the mud in his new set of clothes, mom or babysitter will have to adapt their mindset. Little Johnny might get carted home in a new diaper and not much else. Just like in this example, sometimes the key to creativity and adaptability doesn't require much else than a change of expectation.

5. They engage in physical exercise to stretch themselves (both physically and mentally).

I know what you're thinking: what does achieving mental toughness have to do with how many times a week I go to the gym? Physical exercise is one of the most popular and easiest ways to engage mental toughness.

Remember gym class in high school, when your teacher made you run laps around the gym? When your lungs burned, and your legs felt like jelly, you kept running, partially because your classmates would all see if you stopped, and partially because you wanted to see if you could.

You were training yourself to be mentally tough. Now, as an adult, that manifests like this: doing five reps instead of just doing four. Getting up out of bed and going for a run when you really just want to sleep in the extra thirty minutes.

Pushing yourself to run to that lamppost, and then the next one. The relationship between pushing your body and pushing your mind is strong.

6. They balance their time between training and resting.

Don't mistake mental toughness practice for lack of balance between your goals and rest. Mental toughness isn't devoting all your time and energy, all the time, to attaining your goals. It's about being hyper-focused and persistent in the time you've allotted to work toward your goals. Going full-power all the time will lead to burn-out and stress, neither of which is helpful for growing your mental toughness.

Tips for Mental Toughness:

- When you're struggling with being creative, break out of your normal day-to-day routine. Do something different.

- Use the scenario analysis mental model to start your day. Mentally rehearsing for challenges that may come up will ensure that you are more prepared when these situations do occur.

- Picture yourself achieving your goals and how you will get there. Be honest and realistic in these visualizations. Leave room for setbacks.

- Write your goals down and track your progress. Few things are more motivating than being able to see tangibly how you're moving closer to where you want to be.

- If you end up missing a day or two of your new habit, don't make excuses for yourself and don't beat yourself up. Just get back into it as soon as you can.

- Again, celebrate your victories!

What can you do today to start becoming more mentally tough? Do you know what you want or do you need to sit down and prioritize your goals using some of the mental models we've discussed? Do you know what tasks or habits you want to introduce to your daily routine to accomplish your goals? Do you have an accountability partner who will call you out when you don't accomplish that task?

You can be a person with grit. Your success is up to you and how hard you're willing to work for it. Leave behind the misconception that you're not talented enough or experienced enough, and start believing this: you are already on your way to where you want to end up.

# Conclusion

I thank you once again for downloading this eBook and hope you had a good time reading it. As is apparent, the book's main aim was to propagate the idea of lateral and critical thinking and showing you how you can solve your problems on a daily basis. The idea is to also help you understand the process of problem solving.

Critical thinking itself, as you have learned, comes with several benefits of its own. When you can think critically, you are able to communicate better, which facilitates better relationships with others. This leads to improved happiness and fulfillment. When you are able to think critically, you can identify solutions to problems that you did not realize were as difficult to solve as they were, and you are able to do so without giving up.

Critical thinkers utilize their abilities constantly—you can figure out how to make your decisions, how to interact with others, and why you should think or act in a certain way all because you learned how to think critically. You learned how to consider situations around you in ways that are deliberate, attentive to detail, meticulous, and meant to bring you closer to solving any problems that you have encountered, always managing to make your way to the right decision, even if you have to hit some roadblocks along the way. Nevertheless, when you become a critical thinker, one thing is for sure: You become intelligent, informed, and capable of making judgments that are trustworthy and should be valued by others.

At times you might be the only one facing a problem and might not want everybody to see that you are uncomfortable or are deeply affected by the problem. Problem solving saves the day during such situations. These problems can be large or small but as long as they are helping you to find feasible solutions, you will be required to tackle them with rationality. That is where you will be required to put on your critical thinking caps. Problem solving and critical thinking go hand in hand. It is only when you think creatively or out of the box that you will be able to identify a solution to the problem.

Now that you're clued in to some of the more specific details of escaping negative thinking, reconnecting with yourself, improving your productivity, and solving the problems in your path, you have a good deal of work ahead of you! It's time to *think* about what you want from life and what your goals are. Next, you will want to *do* the things necessary that will help you to *be* all you can be.

Never underestimate a person who makes his decisions based on his own intuition, for those are the people who feel free and justified. Because they are the ones who follow their heart. And now that you have finished reading this book, I bet you have enough knowledge to be one of them as well. However, do keep in mind that in making a decision, you have to be able to achieve balance in using your intuition and facts. Making the best decisions will definitely make life worth living, and you will add a personal touch to every decision by trusting your instincts.

Using the information in these pages to achieve your goals is all we want for you, so please go forward, identify your patterns, outline your goals, work toward them, and achieve the success that we know you're capable of achieving.

Made in the USA
Columbia, SC
23 June 2020